NELSON TIFT
1810-1891

THE COLONEL CAME TO STAY

G.C.G. Vol. II
1836-1842

by

Robert P. Dews

Rebel Books
P.O. Box 302
Edison, Ga. 31746

Copyright 1986 © Robert P. Dews
All Rights Reserved

Library of Congress Catalog Card Number 81-51562
ISBN 0-940184-09-5

Also by Robert P. Dews:
   The Successful Failure
   Mobile East
   Survival at 2500°
   Early Joel I & II (Indexed)
   Whichaway?
   The Georgia-Florida League, 1935-1958, two editions
      The Melody Lingers On
      Extra Innings
   Gentle Connecticut Georgian, Vol. I

Cover Design by J. Nebraska Gifford

Printed in the United States of America

Chapter 1

Things had gone smoothly for Nelson and Charles Tift in the new store in Hawkinsville. The move of all equipment and supplies from the now abandoned town of Hartford had been accomplished with little trouble. The carpenters were still finishing the job of building the new store and outbuildings.

People were sending back to Hartford for the fine spring water they missed so badly. Many thought the water in the new town was causing the sickness they were encountering.

Nelson had decided to accept one of several offers to build a "trading town" on the west bank of the Flint. Charles would replace him at Mr. Gonedy's new store, having joined his brother in Augusta and followed him to Hawkinsville while learning the mercantile business from Nelson. Many of their leisure hours were spent remembering their sailing voyages from Mystic, Connecticut, to Charleston, Savannah, St. Augustine and Key West where their grandfather and father had been prominent in the building of that city.

There was much to be done getting the finishing touches on the new building and seeing that the shelves were stocked with goods. Charles and Nelson were, in turn, down with the fever that had felled others.

"I tell you, Charles, the water we are drinking is making everybody sick because it has this riverbank limestone in it. You can nearly taste the pure mineral. Mr. Gonedy insists that we would be better off to send back to the old spring at Hartford until they can get a deeper well dug here." Nelson grimaced at the taste.

"Well, we had better do something. You know we have two out of the three carpenters in the outhouse all the time during working hours. Everybody in town is having the same problem and most outhouses have been expanded from one to two and, sometimes, three-holers," Charles said in a dead-srious tone.

"Oh, come now, let us not wax morbid on the subject. I am sure that things will get better," Nelson said half-heartedly.

"Sure, it will if we all put our shoulders to the wheel and work for a solution to the problem," the younger brother said, adding, "and wishing won't make it so!!"

Just before leaving for his new assignment, Nelson found out that the offer made by the "silent partner," James Gonedy, was not exactly the same as that being offered him by Holcombe and Peck. The slight difference in their interpretation of what was being offered to Nelson involved the "and found" clause of the offer. The Augusta partners were saying that they would pay Nelson fifteen hundred dollars a year, and "and found", while James Gonedy was saying they were to pay Nelson the same amount of money but that he was to pay for his own living expenses. Of course, this made a vast difference, and Nelson wrote identical letters to both parties asking for further clarification as to which it would be. An answer came by return stage from Holcombe and Peck in Augusta, who stated that they were not overly concerned with the little extra involved as they were much more concerned with getting the best possible man for the job and thought Nelson was that man. But James Gonedy would not back down one inch from his interpretation of the firm's original offer. Nelson wrote another letter to the Augusta partners telling them that he could not go forward with the project unless James Gonedy relented and agreed to go along with Holcombe and Peck's terms.

During the interim between exchanges of letters with the Augusta-based authorities, Mr. John Rawls, Esq., president of the new bank in Hawkinsville, called on Nelson and requested that he consider taking an interest in the management of a town, steamboat, and warehouse on the Flint River in southwest Georgia. "Some call the river 'Lona Tiska Hatchi' and some know it as the 'Thronateska.' Old Benjamin Hawkins, for whom this town is named, was the Indian Agent in Georgia for many years, and he said it was the 'Lona Tiska Hatchi.' At any rate, it is now the Flint River," said the intrepid Squire Rawls. "We will give you free shipping privileges for cotton for one year after the steamboat is delivered."

"Squire Rawls, your proposition sounds exciting, and I certainly want to hear more of the particulars, but I suppose that you are aware that I am already negotiating with another party for a similar venture?"

"Quite so, Mr. Tift. It is your decision to make; however, one word of caution. If you dally too long over your decision, our offer may be withdrawn. In this instance, haste is of the utmost importance."

"I understand and will make a decision and contact you at the bank."

"That James Conedy is the most stubborn mule that I have ever seen, Nelson. From what you told me Mr. Rawls and his constituents won't wait forever for you to make up your mind. I suspect that old Gonedy thinks he has you over a barrel and is holding you off as long as possible by dragging his feet, perhaps making you lose the opportunity to go with the Rawls group. He is holding over our heads that he will let us both go from this job if we lose both the other opportunities," Charles said in indignation.

"That about sums it up, Charles. I think I'd better take the bull by the horns and go see Mr. Rawls to ask if his proposition is still open."

"I say you go to see Mr. Rawls right now," Charles said with intense feeling, knowing full well that Nelson had about made up his mind to go that route anyway. He added, "If you have waited too long and Squire Rawls has another man, and if Mr. Gonedy gets mad and lets us both go, you still have the two thousand from the Augusta sale. I feel sure that Brother William Mercer will let us have enough lumber to build a store here in Hawkinsville, and we can go into business for ourselves."

Nelson went to see John Rawls and was told that the Squire was leaving for Macon by stage within the hour, and if the agreement with Nelson was not signed, sealed and delivered by that time, that he, Rawls, would contact a man in Macon to handle the job. It was now or never for Nelson Tift; he knew that this was the moment of truth for him, that this was the decision on which his whole future—his life—might depend. He said a silent prayer to his God, looked the banker in the eye and said, "Mr. Rawls, I accept your offer!"

"Fine! The papers are drawn up with just the names to be filled in and for all concerned to sign," replied the banker as he handed Nelson a sheaf of official-looking documents. "Read these carefully, Mr. Tift," said Rawls, walking from his office out into the front room of the bank, leaving Nelson alone with the contracts before him. The young man brought his full powers of concentration to bear on the papers before him and studied the agreement, which read:

"Hawkinsville, Georgia, 24 September, 1836. This agreement entered into this day between Nelson Tift, of the first part, and a company consisting of the following individuals of the second part, viz: John Rawls, R. N. Taylor, W. V. King, B. J. and F. J. Watts. Certifieth that the said Nelson Tift of the first part is to receive from the said company of the second part three whole shares and equal interest in three other common stock shares of the following property which comprises 18 shares: one steamboat in complete order intended for the navigation of the Flint River and two lots of land situated on the west bank of the Flint River in Baker County, intended for the location of the town. The said Nelson Tift of the first part shall pay the said company of the second part five hundred dollars or more in proportion to the whole cost for every full share, and the payments shall be as follows: one thousand dollars in cash and the balance within one year from this date with interest until paid. It is further agreed by the parties that the company owning the above 18 shares, comprising the above mentioned property be now organized and known as the Rawls and Tift Company, for the purpose of merchandising, boating, traffic, etc., and that the said Nelson Tift shall have the entire management and conduct of said business, unless otherwise directed by a majority of the stockholders, for one year next ensuing, for which services the said Nelson Tift shall receive from the common stock of the said company, thirteen hundred dollars.

         NELSON TIFT
         JOHN RAWLS
         (for self and others)"

The banker came back into the office and said, "Well, Mr. Tift, what do you think? Have you made your decision yet?"

"Yes, Sir, I am ready to sign the papers and have the one thousand dollars with me to bind the deal," Nelson said, knowing that there was no backing away now that he had given his solemn word.

"Very fine. You sign over your name, and I shall do likewise. Here, let me fill out the receipt there at the bottom of the agreement," John Rawls said as he counted out the money and affixed his signature to the receipt, which read, "Received at Hawkinsville on October 5, 1836, from Nelson Tift, one thousand dollars on three shares of the property specified in a former agreement of September 24, 1836, as per agreement which is part of the whole.

JOHN RAWLS
(for self and others)"

"Well, partner, when can you report to take over the property on the Flint and start building a store and warehouse?" the banker asked.

Nelson did some fast calculating. He had noted that the thousand dollars he had paid the banker would not be a matter of record, according to the official document they had both signed, until the fifth of October. "It may be at least two weeks, maybe the second week in October before I can settle my affairs here and get down there. Will that be soon enough?" He paused, then asked a question that had been bothering him, "How do you suppose I should go about getting down there?"

"Well, you could go by horse, or by wagon, or you could just take the Alligator Stage that runs through here and on down the Blackshear Trail to Fort Early. It stops at Pindertown and there is a ferry near there that you take across the Flint River to the western shore. On the other side of the Flint, you go down river about three miles to where the property that we will build on is located. There is another ferry just below that point, but I am not sure that the stage coach has a stop on the eastern shore where it lands."

"Doesn't the stage run on the west side of the Flint at all?" Nelson asked somewhat nervously.

"I am afraid not, Nelson. Now, let me tell you how much I have been able to find out about the situation down there. Most of what I tell you was told to me by Alexander Shotwell, and I have picked up a little from bank customers who drew land down there through the lottery and have been down to try to locate the land they drew. From what I have been able to gather, the ferry at Pindertown is built where a big creek meets the Flint; in fact, two big creeks, the Kinchafoonee and the Muckalee join and become the Muckafoonee at the Indian town of Philema. This short creek drops over a high ledge and cuts through limestone for about a mile before it reaches the Flint. I understand there is a 'run-around' above this fall line where cotton boxes and small barges can be sucked through and continue on up into the Muckalee and the Kinchafoonee. Now the ferry is owned by the Green Tinsley family, but the Tison men usually run it. The Tisons also own the one below our property farther downstream. Someone at Pindertown will take you down to the ferry, or, if you are on horseback, they will point the way for you. Alexander Shotwell started building the town of Richmond on the flats above the west bank of the Flint where the ferry lands. The fever and mosquitoes drove him out, and he went some distance farther down the river to the spot where we will now build."

"But I don't understand. If Shotwell is there, what are we doing going into his town?" Nelson asked in a puzzled tone.

"Shotwell laid out a town. Later various reasons—the fear of Indian trouble being most paramount and owning so much land that he was becoming land-poor being another, and last but not least, the mosquitoes, bad water, and fever—caused him to abandon the building of the town. And, of course, that is where we came into the plans," the Squire replied.

"What is there that Shotwell left for us to work with?"

"There is nothing but high ground with miles and miles of pines, but it is the head of navigation on the Flint River. Alexander did turn over all of his plans for the town and the results of his surveys of the property; so although there are no buildings or people there, the town has been planned and laid out."

"Mr. Rawls, that Alexander Shotwell really gets around, doesn't he?"

"Alexander is quite a character and a very nice gentleman. Of course, you do know that it was Shotwell who told us about you, or do you?"

"I did meet and have a long talk with the gentlemen, and there has been a slowly budding suspicion in my mind that I was beginning to perceive his fine hand in this whole situation," Nelson answered.

"All right then, Mr. Tift, I think this concludes our business for the day. I must be getting over to catch the stage. I suggest that you see Robert Taylor who will be going down with me to the property after I get back from this trip to Milledgeville and Macon. By the way, I will see Shotwell in Macon. Is there anything I can tell him for you?" the banker asked.

"Yes, Sir, please give him my warmest regards and thank him for letting you people know about me. Tell him that I hope to see him later on the west bank of the Flint," Nelson answered as he shook hands and left the bank.

On the tenth of October, 1836, Charles saw Nelson off on the stage. They went through Slade's, Gay's, Tison's, and on into Pindertown. They went over the Blackshear Trail to Fort Early and arrived in Pindertown on the thirteenth of October, 1836. Pindertown was a cluster of buildings consisting of three stores, a post office, the stage stop, a tavern, and a blacksmith shop. Mr. William J. Ford was the Postmaster, a grey-haired man past middle age, who spoke to Nelson in a friendly manner. "Will you be spending the night before continuing on to Bainbridge or Tallahassee, or do you want to go on to the ferry and across the Flint?"

"Goodness me, how did you know that I was looking for the ferry?" Nelson asked slapping the red clay dust from his hat and coat while trying to stretch some of the stage cramps from his back and legs.

"Well, I ain't no magician, but you ain't from these parts around Pindertown, which might be anyplace ten miles up and down the east bank of the Flint hereabouts. I also asked you if you were going on to Bainbridge or Tallahassee, and all you heard was about the ferry, so I guess you are looking for it. Well, you could be agoing to Danville, Palmyra, Bryon, or Gillionville, and if you stay on the old Hartford Trail, you might be agoing all the way to Fort Gaines where I have kinfolks," the old man laughed and then asked abruptly, "Say, you don't happen to be Nelson Tift, be ye?"

"Why, yes. I am Nelson Tift, but how did you know?" the young man asked in surprise.

William Ford was now very serious. He told Nelson that Robert Taylor and John Rawls had left word several days ago for a traveler by the name of Nelson Tift to be directed to them on the west bank of the Flint where they would be working with the five men that the postmaster had been able to get for them. Robert Taylor had told Nelson that he was going to meet Rawls with a two-horse wagon full of picks, shovels, hammers, saws, broad axes, and other tools. He had three tents, camping supplies, and provisions and left word that they would probably have already come and gone by the time Nelson got down to the property.

"Can you take me down to the ferry, Mr. Ford?" Nelson asked the postmaster. "I have only this one small bag and that little steamer trunk which I hope you will hold here for me until I can come for it."

"Do better than that, Mr. Tift. You can perform a real service for me, too. One of the men that is with the work crew over there has a sick wife and baby, and I need to get him word to come back here as quickly as possible. I'll furnish you with a good horse, and you can send the man back on it. How's that?"

Nelson thanked the postmaster as he mounted the well-behaved mare, and Mr. Ford directed him to a fairly good, sandy, wheel-bearing road that led to Tinsley's Ferry. It was only two miles or so of wandering road through thick forest to the river. Nelson heard the mighty rush of water over what sounded like a waterfall, but when he came into sight of the ferry, this turmoil proved to be a great solid rock shoal just above where the water from a mighty creek joined the rushing Flint River. This would be the junction of the Flint and Muckafoonee Creek that John Rawls had described. The mare picked her way gingerly down to the ferry, and her rider noted that this ferry was attached to the rock banks and great trees on each side of the river and from the solid rock of the "V" where the creek and the river came together by a chain that was attached to the ferry. This gave the necessary flexibility and strength needed when the water was high and swift, and also the potential of settling lower in the water during the dry months.

Two oxen hitched to an apparatus similar to a canegrinding mill furnished the power for the ferry. The animals walked around in an established circle no matter whether the ferry was being towed from east to west or west to east. Only one crude-looking gear had to be set in order to reverse the direction of pull by the powerful beasts.

A well set up, dark-haired, young man puffing on a corncob pipe was taking catfish off his trot line. He finished his task and hurried onto the ferry to motion the traveler aboard.

"Are you Mr. Tinsley?" Nelson asked.

"Nope, and I ain't even Mr. Tison; he is my father. However, we do run the ferry for the Tinsleys and have a smaller one of our own on down river several miles." The sturdy young man laughed, showing strong white teeth, and continued, "I am Charles Tison, and we live just up on the bank a piece." He motioned back towards the bluff on the east side of the river from which they were now pulling away.

"Mr. William Ford said you would point me downstream to where some men are working. Do you know anything about them?" Nelson asked as Charles Tison led his mare off the ferry for him.

"I shore do. Rode down there to see them and the man that runs our little ferry on down from them a way. Them men has shore done some work down there in the short time they have been at it. Now you take the trail to the left after you follow the road that goes straight ahead from the bluff up there. The big road is the Hartford Trail that leads westward to Fort Gaines. The little trail that you are going to take to the left goes on down river to where you want to go. It ain't a bad trail 'cept in the bottoms, and you and the mare will make it on down there to where you can hear them 'aworking 'afore sundown." He handed the reins to Nelson and said, with lowered head and an embarrassed manner, "We charges two bits for a man and his beast."

It was Nelson's turn to be embarrassed, and he quickly said, "Please excuse my manners, Mr. Tison. I was listening to you and watching the crossing so closely that I even forgot to tell you my name. I am Nelson Tift, and I am to be in charge of the town we are going to build downriver. Here, let me give you a little extra as I am taking this mare and a message to one of the men regarding sickness in his family. He will want to get back up here and cross to Pindertown tonight. Will it be convenient for you to wait for him?"

"Mr. Tift, it would be no trouble for me to wait around for him, but he might have a rough time of it trying to get up the river back here in the dark through the woods. Tell him that the man on duty at our ferry down there stays there all night and for him to wake him and go back to Pindertown by the old stage road."

"Thank you so much, Charles Tison. You have been most kind to me, and I hope to see much of you in the future," Nelson said as he led the mare up the rather steep ramp to the Hartford Trail. At the top of the bluff a man and his wife sat in their one-horse wagon waiting to go down to the ferry. Nelson tipped his hat to the woman and spoke to the man and started past them.

"Hey, young feller, where you going? Fort Gaines, or just to Danville, Philema, or Starkesville?"

"Sir, I am going downriver about three miles to meet some friends where we are trying to build a new town," Nelson answered as he looked over the thin, raw-boned man and his bird-like wife who peeped at him from beneath a too-large poke bonnet.

"Well, there ain't nothing down there now 'cept miles and miles of pines and more Injuns that the army rounded up and marched off awhile back," the little man said as he spat tobacco juice at the ground and eased his rig carefully down the ramp to the waiting ferry.

"Thank you for the information, Sir. We will be careful," Nelson called after the wagon and set the mare's head on toward his destination. The trail off to the left was fairly level and free of fallen timbers. Nelson lost sight of the river and followed the trail for over an hour before he heard the sounds of voices, and of the axes being sunk into the timber. He knew then that he had arrived at his destination on the west bank of the Flint River. He said a silent prayer of thanks as he had begun to believe that he had somehow taken the wrong turn and had become lost from the little river trail. Nelson rode on for five minutes or so, then he saw men trimming a great pine that had just been felled.

"Snake her over this way, boys," shouted a man sitting on a horse about fifty yards from the working men. Nelson rode forward to shake hands with Robert Taylor.

"Well, well, Nelson, we have been expecting you. Come on, let's go up to where we are starting the store house with these hewn logs. How was the trip? You didn't ride that mare all the way here from Hawkinsville, did you?"

"I rode the stage to Pindertown, and Mr. Ford lent me the horse. I must find out which of the men Mr. Ford let you have that has a sick wife and baby. They have taken a turn for the worse, and Mr. Ford wants him to start back home on this mare immediately."

"Oh yes, I know the man," Robert said quickly and called one of the men over and talked with him for a moment. Robert then gave him some money, and Nelson turned the mare over to the man, giving him the message that Charles Tison had sent about going across the river and back up the stagecoach road to Pindertown.

"Here, climb on the horse with me, Nelson. No—hand me your bag first—then climb up. Now, you men snake that one in, square it up and notch it, and let's let it be the last one for today."

When they arrived at the camp on the bluff overlooking the Flint River, a figure that Nelson would never have recognized as being the usually immaculately-dressed John Rawls greeted him through a layer of sawdust, red clay, and sweat.

"I'll tell you, boy, you got here none too soon. I have a belly full, and I will not stay in the Godforsaken place one more day or night. Robert, get the wagon. Leave this boy the tools, provisions, and men. Let us go to the stage stop at Pindertown where we can get the stage out tomorrow. We will leave the wagon and team with Mr. Ford, and Nelson can send for it," the banker shouted disgustedly.

"I got here as quickly as I could, Mr. Rawls, and I am sorry if you have been inconvenienced by my not getting here sooner," Nelson said apologetically.

"Oh, it's not you, boy," Robert said resignedly. "We are both too old for this sort of adventure, and everything has happened to old John from a near rattler bite to painful bee stings, dirt, the terrible gnats, and river water fever, but we will have to spend another night and get an early start in the morning."

Three little white tents stood near where they were building the store house of notched logs. Rawls and Taylor walked over the townsite as laid out by Alexander Shotwell the year before. "I like the way he marked off the streets, so straight and wide. I believe we should try to follow this rough map and his general lay-out of the town," John Rawls said as he slapped at the hordes of insects that seemed to be partial to his person. "It is small wonder to me that Shotwell was ready to unload this project on us. You know he was attempting to settle here and sell off the land on the strength of a vague promise by the government that the Indians would be removed."

"But the army did run the Creeks out several months ago, did they not?" Nelson asked.

"Yes, Nelson, they did; but too late for it to do Alexander any good, as he had given up thinking it would ever be accomplished. He was selling thousands of acres of land to anyone who would give him anything at all for choice lands up and down the Flint. He sold to the folks around the little towns of Bainbridge and Newton and to us here at this site," Robert explained. "I guess General Winfield Scott knows that he left pockets of Creek Indians all over southwest Georgia. Some of them had drawn land in the lottery, using the family names of whites with whom they had intermarried. There was a census of sorts taken in this territory in 1820, but there has never been a real census taken of the Indians in these parts and the white families into which these Creeks had either intermarried or with whom they were very close friends. These friends were not about to turn the Indians in to the Army if they did not want to be taken west. So when the army came to each military district, only those who were ready to go were rounded up. Of course, the Creek leaders who were well known to the army and whom the authorities in high places wanted moved west of the Mississippi were among these sent away. The rest simply faded back into the swamps until the army departed the area. Now 'squatters' are moving in and settling on land they think is open for them. It will be interesting to see what happens when the 'real' owners go back to claim the land they drew in the lottery." Robert added, "You know, President Andrew

Jackson, the Georgia Governor, and the Supreme Court might really get into a battle over this very problem."

The men took turns keeping the fire going during the night. The fire seemed to keep the insect activity down a little as well as being a security precaution. Nelson took the watch of the man who had gone back to see about his sick family. Next morning the sun seemed to spring from the tall pines on what promised to be a beautiful fall day. The smoke curled up from the fire where salt pork and wheat-cakes were being cooked. The aroma of the frying meat and boiling coffee had all the men waiting impatiently for the signal to breakfast. One of the men had gone to sleep rolled up in his blanket under the wagon and when awakened during the night for his tour of duty, had found that a large snake had somehow crawled into the bedroll with him. It had fallen out when he got up and threw the covering off himself. "I declare that wuz the maddest snake you ever seen. He wuz a-striking at ever'thing in sight afore he made off down to the river," the man told his laughing fellow workers.

"Nelson, we will take one of the hands to Pindertown with us and send him back with some provisions. We will talk with Mr. Ford about some more help to get the work done here," John Rawls said after they had eaten and preparation had been made for the departure of the two-horse wagon.

"Gentlemen," Nelson said in the formal way he used when getting ready to bring up official business, "I have been thinking about a name for this place we are building. It is obvious that we cannot continue to refer to it as 'the property' forever and must give it an official name that has some meaning and one that people can easily remember."

"Yes, we have been thinking about calling it 'Chehaw' for the big Indian town that was destroyed here by mistake during the Seminole Indian War, but that name has bad memories for all concerned. We thought about calling it 'Shotwell' but ruled that out as it might discourage a prospect from investing here, thinking it to be a lawless place. What name do you suggest, Nelson?" John Rawls asked from the wagon seat where he waited for the wagon to depart for Pindertown.

"Gentlemen, I have an old friend who worked on the great Erie Canal between ALBANY and Buffalo, New York. He has told me much about these cities. Albany, New York, is at the head of navigation on the great Hudson River and from what folks say and the looks of the great rock shoals here and at Tinsley's Ferry, I would say that we are standing at the head of navigation on the Flint River. I suggest we name this place Albany, Georgia," Nelson said.

"Albany, Georgia. Albany, Georgia. Yes, that has a nice ring to it, like the clapper hitting a clear-sounding bell. Yes, I think we should call the head of navigation on the Flint, Albany, Georgia," agreed Robert Taylor, and turning to the impatient John Rawls he asked, "What do you think, John?"

"Amen!" answered that worthy, slapping at the horde of black gnats and mosquitoes that hung around his dust-stained tall hat like a halo, "But come on Robert; let's get out of here before these little winged devils eat us alive."

Chapter 2

Nelson and the three laborers watched the men in the two-horse wagon disappear into the pines and turned to the job at hand. "Let's put up the logs we have notched and go get some more," Nelson said, conscious that this was his first order given at the new townsite this fourteenth day of October, 1836, They worked all day long, and that evening as they sat around the camp-fire, the men agreed that they had this day made great progress, but that they needed more help. They were doing the work of men and animals all day. Nelson agreed with them when they said, "It is not the cutting, notching, and squaring of the timbers that is killing us. It is the work that we are doing that the mules or oxen should be doing that is taking up much of our time as well as breaking our backs and spirits."

"Mr. Tift, you wanna go down and hit the water with us after we get a bite to eat?" one of the men asked.

"Yes, thank you. I think that would really help us all. When we get back here to the fire, you men turn in for the night. I have lots of figuring to do here by the light of the fire, and after I get through, I will awaken one of you for the next watch."

It proved to be a long, cold, lonely vigil and the fire seemed a close friend to the young man sitting by it with his writing materials in his lap, writing, figuring, and listening to the black bear, cougar, bob cat, deer and some of the smaller creatures as they hung around the perimeter of the firelight. Every now and then he heard the flat, loud warning "crack" of the beaver, hitting the water with his mighty tail. The angry roar of the bull alligators and the unceasing chorus of the frogs filled the dark night around him. Once, just for a brief moment, the small birds stopped their nervous twittering and became still.

The symphony of the frogs subsided into a muted lullaby, the movement of the animals ceased, and Nelson had the distinct feeling that a human being was there outside the circle of firelight looking intently at him. The hair rose on the back of his neck as he tried to remember everything that he had ever been told about Indians for he was sure that it must be Indians out there. Who else could creep through the woods and get this close to the fire without startling the animals into an audible flight from the area? Whatever or whoever it was out there had just emerged among them without alarming them, causing only an alert silence.

Nelson tried to act as if he were not alarmed and went about doing what a person does around a campfire when he thinks he is alone. He kept making notes on the paper before him, pausing now and then to put another stick on the fire. After about an hour of silence, the birds began their chirping again, and the animal activity resumed. The frogs started their croaking—whatever had crept silently into the edge of the circle of light had departed just as unobtrusively. Soon it was false dawn and then, as the sun rose, the other men began to stir themselves. Another day had begun.

For one full week, every day, "can-see-to-can't-see" hours were worked by everyone. The wagon had been brought back by a brother of the man who had gone to his sick wife and child. Work had proceeded at an accelerated pace with the big wagon, the team of oxen to do the backbreaking work, and one more man to share the remaining tasks. The store had been completely covered, and Nelson was elated with their first week's work. He decided to pay the men off and drive them back to Pindertown for a visit with their families. They would all return on Monday morning to the work site, fully refreshed and ready for another week's work. The men were overjoyed to hear of the plan, but Nelson made the mistake of letting them see him juggling his funds around to make ends meet when paying them off.

William Ford invited Nelson to stay at his home and have supper with him Saturday night. Sunday morning church services were well-attended under a great water oak beside the post office. The fall weather was clear and not very cold, the wind just strong enough to keep the last of the summer's gnats and other insects away from the worshipers. Nelson counted twenty-five hardy souls at the services and noted that about one-fourth of them were black. A circuit rider preached the sermon and led the singing afterwards, and then it was time for dinner-on-the-grounds. Never had the boy from Connecticut enjoyed a sermon, singing, and the bountiful supply of food so much. His joy proved to be short-lived as three of his men came up to him after dinner to say that duties at their small farms at this time of the year would prevent them from going back to the building site with him.

"Can you help me get some men to replace you?" Nelson asked them.

"I don't think so. We all pitch in and help one another during crop-gathering time, and if we don't harvest the crops quickly, the rains might set in, and we would lose everything and have to face a winter out here in the middle of nowhere with nothing," their spokesman answered.

"Well, I aimed to tell you'all that ye was arunning awful close to harvest-time, so I ain't exactly s'prised t'hear they told you they cain't go back wid ye," Mr. Ford told Nelson when informed what had happened. "They's no use trying t'other 'round here neither. They's all in d'same boat but ye're welcome to stay here 'til ye can get word to y'r partners in Hawkinsville, or ye can go on to Hawkinsville on the stage tomorrow, and I'll be glad to take care of the animals whilst ye're gone."

Nelson caught the stage out of Pindertown and arrived in Hawkinsville on Wednesday. He found Robert Taylor out of town and John Rawls said brusquely that he had his own problems and did not want to talk about those of Nelson's.

"But, Mr. Rawls, I can't build a warehouse or anything else without some help! Surely you can help me get two or three carpenters or some skilled laborers to take back with me!" Nelson pleaded, although he sensed that he was beating a dead horse in this instance.

"Mr. Tift, I think that if you will read your copy of our agreement that you will find it does not stipulate that I will have anything to do with furnishing the labor to erect a warehouse. That, Sir, is your responsibility."

It was useless to argue the point further, and Nelson returned to where Charles was waiting. "Is old skin flint going to get you some more help, Nelson?" the younger brother asked.

"Not so you can tell it! I just don't know exactly what to do at the moment," Nelson said, and added, "but I'll tell you one thing I do know. You had better hang onto that good-paying job I got you as long as you can or until things get better for me on this Flint River project." He laughed a bitter little laugh and then concluded, "If worse comes to worse, I might have to fall back on you for help this time." They turned and started toward the store just as the banker came out of his office and motioned Nelson to come back over.

"Wait for me at the store. Looks like he is either going to fire me, or he has relented," the older brother said, as he crossed the street to where the banker stood waiting.

Squire Rawls had thought it over and was now ready to concede that he had been a little hasty with Nelson because of the same kind of troubles he was experiencing in Hawkinsville. He advanced Nelson some money for his personal use and five hundred dollars to be used to pay as much as one dollar a day for labor. After reporting the good news to Charles, Nelson sat down and wrote his brothers in Key West asking for them to talk with Brother Hawkins to see if they could influence him to take passage to Apalachicola and from there up the river to the town site at the head of navigation on the Flint. He explained that it would be better to take a steamer to the little port of Bainbridge, Georgia, and continue from there by the Aligator Stagecoach to Pindertown. Nelson wrote Asa how badly he needed Brother Hawkins and let Amos know that he was sympathetic with his domestic difficulties and was praying that this trouble would pass.

"It is not only that I need Hawkins as the master carpenter and dedicated friend that he is. I need him more for being a native Georgian who will be able to open doors for me with these rough frontiersmen who jokingly call themselves 'Crackers'," he wrote. "I find this term 'Cracker' used by many people of diverse backgrounds and most of them say the term means either the 'cracking' of the bullwhip over the lead ox's head when whipping up a team of oxen. Others say that it refers to settlers on the frontier having to get up at the 'cracker' (crack of) dawn to get all their chores done before they go to the fields or the woods for the day's remunerative work."

The brothers talked with the postmaster at Hawkinsville who told them that it would be better for the letter to go by ship via Savannah rather than by Aligator Stage to Tallahassee where it would wait for a stage to Apalachicola, going from there by boat to Key West.

"This will leave by stage today and possibly be in Key West one week from today if it goes straight to Savannah and then down the Atlantic coast to the Keys," he told them.

The stage to Pindertown left bright and early the next morning. Charles saw his brother off. James Gonedy came with them to the stage stop and told Nelson that he bore no grudge against him for accepting the offer of the bank to go to southwest Georgia. Charles was doing a fine job for them in Hawkinsville and could stay with them as long as he wanted to, provided that business warranted his retention with the firm. There were three men and a woman on the stage when Nelson boarded. Two of the male passengers were going all the way to Tallahassee. They were Spanish gentlemen who spoke very little English but talked incessantly to each other in their native tongue. The first overnight stop was at Slade's stagecoach tavern where the accommodations were so crude as to be almost non-existent.

Several rough, rowdy drunks made it impossible for anyone to go to sleep during the early hours of the night, even if the new arrivals could have ignored the terrible stench of the place that had drawn every fly and mosquito in the general area into the tavern. Nelson went out on the sagging front porch to get away from the "pigsty" that the drunks had made of the middle of the room where the men were supposed to sleep. The unhappy husband of the sick woman passenger followed him out into the night. Nelson did not know what to say to the poor creature so he remained silent. After a while the man spoke to him, "Young man, she can't go on like this; we are in a living hell!" He buried his head in his hands, his shoulders began to shake, and Nelson was torn between embarrassment at seeing the stranger cry and his compassion for another human being who was going through a very trying time.

"How long has she been this way, my friend?" Nelson asked. He patted the man on the shoulder in an effort to comfort him. Between sobs that nearly tore him apart the man told Nelson of an unbelievable journey he was making seeking a cure for his beloved wife. They were from Milledgeville. The physicians there had given up on the woman, saying that she would die of consumption and there was little they could do for her. Then an older doctor told them that he had heard of a woman who said she had been cured by a strange man of Irish descent who lived on a river north of Tallahassee. The old doctor had explained that the mysterious healer was not a "real" doctor but one who brought his strange powers from the "Old Country" and combined them with those of his two black and two Indian "wives." The man told Nelson that he and his wife had searched out the "cured" woman, and she had given them instructions on how to find this mysterious "Healer" who lived somewhere north of Tallahassee on a river.

Nelson talked with the man, who said his name was Abe Browne, nearly all night. He told Browne who he was and what he was trying to do down on the Flint. Shortly before dawn they shook hands, both feeling a little better for having unburdened themselves a little to a fellow human being in trouble. The drunks had left the tavern and the two men could now lie down and get an hour or so rest before the stage was ready to resume the journey. Nelson was conscious of the crickets and little animal sounds, the constant moaning of the wind as it sighed through the tall pines and at last, nothing until he heard the stage being brought around. They made several stops that morning, but Nelson noted that Mrs. Browne made no attempt to get out of the stage and make her customary dash to the bushes. Browne gave her a pill and some water from his flask. Nelson noted that the woman's whole lips were compressed in an even thinner line than usual and that she made no movement towards brushing back the stray strands of hair that fell from her bonnet and down across her pinched face. Her hat slid sideways on her head and then Nelson noted that the formerly very neat woman no longer cared or knew that she was getting very untidy. She was a deathly chalk white when they stopped at Gay's Station. Mr. Browne looked over at Nelson and motioned that he needed him. Nelson helped get the little woman out of the stage and into the tavern where she died quietly within minutes. Mrs. Gay and two other women prepared the body for its trip back to Milledgeville, and Nelson secured some lumber and built a suitable coffin for the body. The would strap the coffin on top of the north-bound stage when it came through in the morning. It was all they could do.

Abe Browne took his loss with true Christian serenity. It hurt, and hurt deeply, but he told Nelson that none of their children believed their mother would ever complete the trip but that he had wanted to let her have the only chance there seemed to be for her to get well. As the south-bound stage was getting ready to pull out, Browne came over to Nelson and said, "God bless you, Son. You are a good man. Thank you from the bottom of my heart for all your kindness and concern."

William Ford met the stage when it pulled up in front of his place in Pindertown. "Nelson, I have three men here. They are all carpenters by trade and have their own tools. One is from Newton, one from Starksville, and the other was on his way down to the new town of Bainbridge to do some work, but I think I have talked him into working with you." Nelson felt like hugging and kissing the old man as this news came at a time when he was feeling the weight of the world on his shoulders, and now he felt that most of this weight had suddenly been released. The three men already had their baggage and tools in the wagon. Nelson talked with them for a moment, and they agreed on two dollars a day and "found" as their wages.

"You can pass the word that we will give one dollar to ordinary laborers," Nelson told the new carpenters as they made their way down to the ferry. A very loquacious old fellow known for the thousands of stories which he freely dispensed to his customers introduced himself to Nelson saying, "Mr. Tift, I be the father of Charles Tison. He told me about yore town downriver, and I went down there yesterday, and Man, them blacks and that big half-breed you left in charge has shore done a fine job of clearing and burning that plateau off." Nelson started to ask a question of the old man, but he had digressed to another long spiel about his Indian fighting days in Florida with Andy Jackson. When he got to the other side and turned to pay old man Tison, Nelson started again to ask about the big half-breed and his black helpers but did not want to appear absolutely unaware of what was going on down at the town, so refrained from showing his ignorance. "Give my regards to your son, and you both come down and visit us, Mr. Tison," Nelson said as he paid the talkative oldster.

When they arrived at the site, Nelson found it hard to believe his eyes. Mr. Tison had not been exaggerating when he had told how much work had gone on since Nelson had left to go to Hawkinsville. Half of the area laid out by Shotwell had been cleared and neatly trimmed logs lay alongside the "streets." Smoke still rose from some of the fires that were burning the limbs trimmed from the fallen timbers. One of the men, the one called Stovall, from Starksville, came over to where Nelson was standing staring around in amazement and said, "Mr. Tift, you act like all this is a big surprise to you. Mr. Ford said you had some partners. Maybe they somehow got this labor down here without you knowing about it."

"Stovall, call Hall and Dollar over here. I have been to Hawkinsville begging my partners for some men and was turned down. I don't have any more idea about what has happened here than you'all do," Nelson said emphatically.

Hall, the cabinet maker from Newton, spoke up and said, "Old man Tison said something about a big half-breed working some blacks here and getting this area cleared. Now I know that folks do talk and tell tales about such things; but for what it's worth, I heard that when a very few folks were trying to clear the land and build Newton, the high water drove them out. They near 'bout gave up on the project, and it was more than a month before they went back to see if they could salvage some of their tools. Well, you can imagine their amazement when they found their tools neatly cleaned and stacked and all the work done, clean as a whistle — kinda like what we found here."

"I am not one to look a gift horse in the mouth, and there will probably be a plausible explanation of all this later, but it looks like we have enough trees felled and trimed to keep us busy for a month without cutting down another tree. Come on. Let's get unloaded and find out who is the best cook in the crowd," Nelson said as they started unloading and getting ready for the night which was fast falling.

One week after returning to the site with the new carpenters, the store house had been completed, a sixteen-by-twenty-foot bunkhouse had been built, and the timbers had been laid for a forty-by-one-hundred-foot warehouse. Nelson put two men to work on a special project, and in two days they produced a flat-bottom boat eight feet wide and fifteen feet long. He showed them how to use oakum made from rope and how to caulk the seams with resin from the pine trees. After they had finished the job, they put heavy rocks inside the boat and submerged it beneath the water. After three days they brought the boat up; the wood had swelled and closed all leaks. The new boat gave them a sense of security and independence as well as being a great help in getting their work done in and around the river.

Young Charlie Tison came down several times to talk with Nelson and the men. He said that his folks had moved into the area shortly after the Jackson treaty had opened the country for whites. Nelson asked if any boats came up as far as Tinsley's Ferry. "No, Siree!" said young Tison emphatically as he spat brown tobacco juice at a doodlebug pushing his load along through the powdery dust. "Why, the water would have to be at flood stage for a steamboat or a big barge between here and Fort Early, and we would have to pull our ferry up out of the water and release the chains. Some have built boats up at the old Creek Agency and brought them downstream, but in each case they have had to wait until flood stage to get them downstream from here to Fort Early. Why, it's even a mite of trouble getting a steamer from Bainbridge up to this point when the water is at normal stage, and it is next to impossible when the drought is on and the river low. Hell's Gate is awful dangerous, and the Flint River is really something wild where the big Itchaway-Notchaway Creek runs into the Flint down below Newton. Spring Creek comes into the Flint just before it joins the Chattahoochee and forms the Apalachicola. 'Course, Hell's Gate is just one of the bad spots as there are shoals, rocks, sand bars, and snags to be watched out for at all times. One of the worst is 'Devil's Rocks' where General Edmund P. Gaines lost all the provisions and equipment that he was taking to his commander, Andrew Jackson, in 1818. Now, my Pa says that this place you call Albany is the true head of navigation on the Flint, but there's a heap of folks at Newton and Bainbridge as might dispute the claim."

"Mr. Tison, have you ever heard of a big half-breed with a band of blacks and half-breeds who live around this area?" Nelson asked cautiously.

"Mr. Tift, Mr. Tison is my Pa. I am Charlie Tison. To answer your question, you must be speaking of Moses who runs things over to the old Indian settlement on the Kinchafoonee Creek at Kinnard's Landing and cowpens. Well, Jack Kinnard was a friend of Moses' father, who was a famous Indian war chief. The present Kinnard out at Kinnard's landing is William, the nephew of old Jack. Like the Kinnards before him, William is friendly to the settlers and is well educated according to the standards of these parts. 'Course, this is all camp-fire talk, but my old man says he fought with and against Moses' father and knowed Jack Kinnard. Pa made a trip with him from the trading post down through Fort Gaines to Pensacola to the main Panton and Leslie Trading Post and back to Kinnard's landing." Charles thought a minute, then asked, "But how come you asked about Moses?"

"I would appreciate it if you would call me Nelson, and I will call you Charlie. We are about the same age and this using 'Mister' every time we speak is most awkward. Now that we have that settled, I want you to look around and see the work that we have accomplished because of the fact that this Moses and his men came in during my absence and did much clearing and cutting of timbers for us. I would like for you to tell your father to thank Moses for me the next time he sees him or his friend William Kinnard. He should tell them that they have our eternal gratitude for the tremendous boost their contribution has given our humble town."

"I shore will, Nelson; that is, I'll get them word of that part of your little speech that I can understand. You talk with too many fancy words sometimes for us folks here on the Flint to follow," Charlie said slowly.

After Charlie Tison had departed, Nelson thought over what he had said about him and his manner of speaking and resolved to try to speak and think with the people here in Albany rather than speak to them. He must try to adjust his thinking so it would be better suited to frontier life rather than the drawing rooms of Augusta, Charleston, or Savannah. This was the same sort of thing that his father had blamed him for, and, once more, he resolved never to be the kind of person who would look down on a man for his lack of an educational background nor look up to any man just because he happened to have impressive educational credentials.

Work was progressing on the big warehouse. Word had gone out that he was paying an exorbitant wage of one dollar a day for labor. By the time he was ready to raise the posts and girders for the large building, enough labor was available for the three-day period necessary to get that portion of the heavy work done.

Squire Rawls wrote Nelson on 19 December, 1836, telling him that he would have to hasten to get title to lot number 323 from Mr. Clayton as there might be trouble from a third party regarding claim to that property. Rawls also said that cotton was down to fourteen-and-a-half cents a pound. But the good news he saved for last: their steamboat had left Apalachicola and would go on up out of that river into the Chattahoochee and to Fort Gaines. It would then come back downriver and enter the Flint to come up to Albany. Rawls stated that he had sold fourteen hundred dollars' worth of lots at one hundred fifty dollars for middle lots and two hundred dollars for corner lots. A steamer, their own, on its way to Albany and people actually buying town lots to build on! These were magic words to Nelson. He knew that they had a long way to go and that much sweat, toil, and tribulations lay ahead, but here, at last, was tangible evidence that they were moving forward and that people other than he and his partners were vitally interested in what they were doing.

It had been raining for a solid week, and the river was rising. Nelson knew that some of the up-river farmers would be able to float their cotton boxes and small barges down to him when the river got a little higher. Nelson would hold their cotton until the barges that he had purchased from the Bond brothers were ready and their steam boat had arrived to take the cotton and other cargo down to the bay at Apalachicola. Boards were being sawn out of logs to be fitted as flooring for the store. Much cotton was already stored in the warehouse, and a large ditch had been laboriously dug from the river landing to the warehouse so that cotton boxes and other containers or small barges and loads of cargo could be floated to the warehouse rather than be man-handled several times in movement from water to warehouse storage. Nelson had done much of the digging of the "ditch" and had found out that he simply could not do such back-breaking work without eating meats, fish, and other heavy foods like those the other laborers ate. It was one thing to make high-sounding resolutions when one sat back and directed the physical efforts of others or, as the hands put it: "to play the role of a sweet back." He found that even the strongest resolutions faded in the glare of reality and the necessity to work and endure in this harsh atmosphere of survival of the fittest as he realized that the key to that survival was physical strength and endurance. Nelson was now working three black hands that he had rented from a Mr. Williams of Danville, and the master carpenter, Hall, of Newton who had elected to stay with him.

Each evening after work, Nelson, Mr. Hall, and the three blacks went downstream in their flat-bottomed boat to the little ferry operated by the Tisons. They fished on the way down; the blacks were expert fishermen and looked forward to this trip in the evenings. They usually had a nice string of bream, bass, catfish, and a sturgeon or two by the time they got to the ferry. They cooked over an open fire on a sandspit where the ferry landed on the east side of the river. On one particular evening Nelson received a pleasant surprise when they got to the ferry. A tall, white-haired man whom he recognized from over a hundred yards away was waving at them, and a powerful voice drifted to them across the water, "Nelson, it's me, Brother Hawkins," the echo of the voice bounced back and forth from bank to bank of the river, and a growing sense of security enveloped Nelson as it sank in that the competent old man had come to help him.

"Who in the world is that hollering at you from over there?" Hall asked, pointing to the big man now standing knee deep in the water just off the sandspit.

"Mr. Hall, that old man is just like a father to me and taught me much of the little I know. That is my dear friend, Brother Hawkins, who has, God knows how, gotten here from

Key West, Florida. Mr. Hall, this old man is so gentle that you will hardly ever hear him give a direct order. That is not the way he works, but he does get the job done, and his word will be the law in Albany." Nelson guided the boat into the landing where Hawkins pulled the bow up on the sand.

"Nelson, boy, you are a sight for sore eyes. I came up on the 'Mary Emeline' from Apalachicola Bay, but they were going on up to Fort Gaines, so I caught a little boat to Bainbridge. There, some folks told me that steamers seldom went any farther north but that I could get a stagecoach to Pindertown which they had heard was across from the new town being built on the west bank of the Flint River. I waited until the next day for the stage, and here I be," the old timer said as he helped Nelson out of the boat.

"Brother Hawkins, I am so glad to see and have you here. When did you get my letter?"

"Asa brought it over to the 'yards' about ten days after you sent it from Hawkinsville. We talked it over, and they knowed I was acoming anyhow if you needed me, so I caught the next thing starting for Apalachicola."

"But what are you doing here at this ferry instead of the one at the stage stop at Pindertown?"

"Well, I had got pretty well acquainted with the driver, who it just so happens, has a cousin who married a cousin of mine. I was setting with him when we stopped at the prettiest place I ever seed. It's not too far from here, and everybody went with him down into the woods a little spell, and there before us was the prettiest jewel that the good Lord ever created a perfect setting for. Nelson, it was a big blue spring, so big that it flows like a blue river from the 'boil' down to the Flint River. The big hole in the ground that this granddaddy of all springs comes from must be fifty feet deep and clear as a bell. Why, a man could build a double pen log cabin down in there where that water comes gushing up from and nary log in that cabin would touch the sides of that cavern. The big oak trees, all hanging with Spanish moss, grow in clusters around the spring. I'll tell you, Son, it be the prettiest place a mortal ever seed."

"Is the water good to the taste? Did the driver and the other passengers drink from it?" the ever-practical Nelson wanted to know.

Old Hawkins searched for the proper words, "Nelson, I declare if they throwed a dying man in that cold water, it would bring him back to life, and I ain't never tasted no better in all my days."

"Mr. Hall, this is my very dear old friend, Brother Hawkins, late of Key West but originally from the Savannah area. Brother Hawkins, shake hands with Mr. Hall of Newton, who has been my mainstay on the job here at Albany," Nelson said and then addressed himself to Mr. Hall, "I guess you might as well get one of the hands busy cleaning the fish and mixing the corn bread. Look after things while Brother Hawkins and I take two of the boys with us as paddlers while we make a quick trip downstream and back before dark." They got back into the boat after it had been unloaded and the two hands pushed off downstream. Nelson told them, "Boys, we are going down to where the big blue creek flows into the river. We will follow the creek up to where Mr. Hawkins will show us this beautiful place he has told us about." The river twisted its way southward, the banks were pockmarked limestone through and out of which the river had cut sheer banks. The great magnolia trees, the ghostly sycamores, the weeping willows, the sturdy cedars, the great hardwood trees of oak, gum, poplar, basswood, hickory, ash, and walnut framed the banks of the rivers while always in the background were the majestic pines. The "hands" pointed out the 'gator slides where the big 'gators sunned and slide down into the water when alarmed or used as a quick path to their intended but unsuspecting prey. Most of the big meat-eaters were now in their winter quarters in caves back up under the limestone banks of the river. "Brother Hawkins, you never did say why you left the stage before it got to the stop at Pindertown," Nelson remarked.

"Oh, I disremembered to answer that question, Nelson. This driver that I was telling you about said he was from over to a place called Isabella, which he said is straight west from here about twenty miles or thereabouts. He claimed the town was named by the Spanish and that several towns in these parts still is called by the names the Spanish give 'em when they was here. They have names like Cuba, Havana, Milan, Elmodel, Eldorendo, and sech and all. Anyway, he said that it was a heap closer to get where I was going if I got off here and took the ferry across to the west bank. In fact, he told me that his boss said that they was thinking about putting a stage stop and a mail drop right across from where you'all is building," the old man ended on a triumphant note. This last statement by Hawkins was music to Nelson's ears as he had written several letters to the "powers that be" in Washington City about this very thing, and he knew that Lott and "General" Warren had been pursuing the same goal. Many had been the dark nights that he had laid aside the journal in which he had been recording the days events and had written both friendly and business letters to people about the mail situation. Now, if and when new citizens started coming in to Albany, he would push for the stage to run on the west side of the river so that Albany could have its own post office and stage stop. As they drifted down towards the blue springs, Nelson recognized that this was farther than he had ever been down the river from Albany. There were two more bends and three straightaways, and then there was the beautiful big blue creek flowing smoothly into the Flint. Brother Hawkins steered them up into the creek, and the men started poling upstream instead of using their paddles. Nelson could see large fish everywhere as they darted from under the long rope-like ferns that swayed in the swift, clear, blue water. Never had he seen anything so quietly beautiful. There was absolutely no sound except that of the twittering birds as the men poled the boat against the current. Hawkins cupped his big hands and drank of the water; Nelson did the same, and then the "hands" followed suit. All tasted and smiled their approval of the good, clean, cold taste of the water. They rounded the last bend and there ahead, framed by the grey Spanish moss like the border of a beautiful old picture was the place so spectacular in its majestic beauty that the old man's words had failed him when he tried to describe it. They paddled over to the edge of the "boil" and gazed down into its incredibly clear depths far below the boat. All manner of fish swam lazily around and into the mysterious mouth of the cave that seemed large enough to conceal a two-horse wagon. Nelson slid out of his shirt and trousers and held his breath as he slid over the side of the boat and into the water. He had prepared himself for a sudden change of temperature but he had just not steeled himself enough; his breath was literally taken from him by the sudden shock of the unbelievably cold water. He swam over the "boil" and found that it would be impossible to drown at that spot unless one had heavy weights attached around his neck or feet, as the water gushed upward with such force. Nelson climbed back into the boat, shivering like a wet dog, and Brother Hawkins quickly handed him his clothes.

After his teeth had ceased their chattering and the boat was gliding back down the creek from the blue spring toward the river, Nelson said, "Thank you so much for sharing this beautiful place with me, Brother Hawkins. It is even more impressive than you led me to believe. Now we must hurry on to the river and get back to the others before it gets too dark." The men waiting at the little ferry had been getting worried as the sun dropped behind the tall pines and night approached. All was ready, and the hungry men had soon eaten their fill, cleaned up, and told the "hand" who ran the ferry that they would see him tomorrow. It was dark going back upriver to the foot of the newly-named Broad Street. This was where they kept the boat and hoped the steam ship would be able to land and turn around as this seemed to be the ideal spot for their "landing" if it proved to be suitable for that purpose. There was just no way to tell until the "Mary Emeline" arrived at Albany. The new moon was just rising when they came around the bend and pulled the boat up through the canal to the warehouse.

Brother Hawkins, after getting himself settled at the store and looking around over the project, said, "Nelson, you have done a real good job of this work on the store, warehouse, and all and such! Well, there might have been one or two things that I would have did 'nother way, but I have to say that we got the start of a good town here."

"Brother Hawkins, I have so many other things I should be doing: trying to contact farmers to sell to them, contracting to buy and ship their cotton and other produce, as well as getting to the real business of buying and selling land. Now you can free me for these most important activities. You build the buildings, and I will build the business."

"Oh, I was told all this by Amos Chapman, just like you said it just now. You give me a hint as to how you want it did, and it will be did that way," the old salt allowed, and asked, "Say, what you got over there in them pens? Looks like some old 'possoms."

"That's right. Mr. Hall traps them now and then, and we have one for supper occasionally. I must say I find them extremely delicious," Nelson replied.

"You do? Why, you don't eat no meat, Boy!" Brother Hawkins was quick to point out.

"Maybe the little Nelson Tift you knew didn't eat meat, but the one standing here in Albany, Georgia, talking to you sure knows that one has to eat meat to survive and work the way we do here on the frontier." Nelson laughed as he saw the look of disbelief on the face of his old friend.

More and more strangers were beginning to show up in the new town; some were land speculators, some prospective merchants; some were land owners who found the land fertile in a great perimeter around Albany. Some bought town lots on Broad, Pine, Jackson, Front, and Washington streets. Most of the newcomers were quite interested in the two barges that lay at the foot of Broad Street ready to make the trip down to Apalachicola Bay as soon as the "Mary Emeline" arrived. "We might hear her steam whistle any day now," Nelson told the others.

Brother Hawkins had assured Nelson time and again that the "Mary Emeline" was a good, sound steam boat. "Son, she do have power enough to handle them big barges there on reasonable waters. She will handle them as long as her steam is up," he added knowing full well that river boats were notorious for having their boilers blow up, running aground, and running into other everyday hazards that were part of the routine and risk of operating on these southern rivers.

Chapter 3

Two days later, along about mid-afternoon, there was an unearthly shriek from downriver. All for miles dropped whatever they were doing to turn their attention and ears downstream and listen. The shriek came again, truly ear-splitting and closer now. Brother Hawkins slapped his thigh and yelled, "It be the 'Mary Emeline.' I'd know that whistle anywhere, anytime! She has done made Hell's Gate and passed by Newton and Devil's Rocks and well on her way here!"

Nelson climbed up on the roof of the store. "You get on the east end of the warehouse," he told Hall. "How long before you think she will get here, Brother Hawkins?"

" 'Bout hour and a half afore we see her tied up down there at the foot of Broad Street where you say the landing ought to be," Hawkins said, "but you better come on down off 'yore perch and make sure the animals and the blacks don't spook when she come in here to land. If they ain't never seen nor heard a steamboat at close quarters you shore better get 'em tied up to something stout 'cause they's gonna bolt surer than taxes, death, and tarnation."

Nelson climbed down sheepishly from the roof. Of course, he should have known these things and should have been making the proper preparations for the "Mary Emeline." Certainly he could not have her captain come looking for him on roof tops. How thankful he was that this wise old man had come to steady and advise him in times like these and to be at his side when decisions were to be made and orders given to get the work done!

"Please talk with the blacks and explain to them about seeing that the animals are properly secured before the 'Mary Emeline' gets here, Brother Hawkins, and please get Mr. Hall down off the warehouse roof and explain that I was excited and should never have asked him to go up there in the first place when there are so many things that he should be supervising both now and after the steamer gets here."

A large group of people had appeared on the east side of the river across from the Albany landing. There were several wagons, one man on horseback, and even one pretty buggy with a man and a woman in it. There was another ear-piercing screech from downstream, and Brother Hawkins estimated it to be from the blue spring area. People were now beginning to appear out of the piney woods, and by the time that they could see the black smoke rising from the approaching "Mary Emeline," horses were getting away from their drivers and running wild down the streets, their masters in full pursuit. Now the smoke could be seen pouring from the red and black painted smokestack, and one man in the crowd of about twenty people clustered around the landing was heard to say, "Man, I can read the 'Mary Emeline' painted in black letters on the white background. Man, ain't she purty?" The cheers from both sides of the river floated out to the Captain and his crew as the stately-looking little steamboat eased into the Broad Street landing with one of the crew members cautiously measuring the water ahead of the vessel with a long pole. The "Mary Emeline" was soon sitting exactly at the foot of Broad Street, and her ropes were thrown ashore to waiting and willing hands that quickly tied her to the large sycamore trees along the shore.

Captain Watts, who was a part owner of the "Mary Emeline" as well as her master, was the first to come down the gangplank. Nelson was waiting with outstretched hand and introduced himself to the Captain.

"Nelson Tift, I am glad to meet you and to assure you and your partners that your town of Albany is truly the head of navigation for the Flint River. I must warn you, young Sir, she is no picnic from Bainbridge up to this point, and from what I can see from here upstream, this is as far as the 'Mary Emeline' can possibly go except possibly in flood stages," said the captain.

"Welcome to Albany, Captain Watts. The people on both sides of the river join me in bidding you welcome on this auspicious occasion. We are a modest settlement now, but with the arrival of ships such as the 'Mary Emeline' and people such as you and your crew members, Albany will soon become a place of some importance," Nelson said loudly so that people on both sides of the river could hear him. Cheers came from both sides of the river and from several small boats full of people coming downstream to greet the steamer.

The word went out, and it was good. Albany was the head of navigation; she was a town with a store, several houses, a big warehouse, two barges, and now her very own steamboat. Cotton was brought in by anxious farmers who had watched the big warehouse being built, the canal being dug, the coming and repairing of the barges, the store opened, land being bought and sold, and other buildings and houses springing up along the shady, wide streets of the ambitious little town. Now, with the arrival of the "Mary Emeline" they knew that at last they had this window on the world, this access to the sea, and that they could and would take the fruits of their labor to markets all over the world. God had been good to His people. Later that night as they sat and talked on deck of the "Mary Emeline," the old Captain offered Brother Hawkins and Nelson some refreshment, saying, "Shall we indulge ourselves to a little Spiritus vini rectificatus, gentlemen?" as he was on his way back to his cabin to get glasses for his guests.

"What do he mean, son?" Old Hawkins asked Nelson guardedly.

"Oh, that is his way of offering us some wine. He does not really talk like that; it is just a Latin phrase he has memorized, I suspect," Nelson said with a chuckle.

During the course of the evening, Nelson discussed leaving one of the barges at Hell's Gate on a future trip to the Gulf so that cotton from that area where the Itchaway-Notchaway flowed into the Flint could be taken aboard for shipment to Apalachicola. "We could pick up much-needed cargo at Apalachicola and bring it back on the return trip," Nelson told the captain.

"I don't think it will be too hard to 'beach' a barge at Hell's Gate, Nelson. More than likely, we will beach them both if the old gully-jumper Notchaway is up to its usual tricks when we go through it. But, seriously though, I do think we can get one into place down there with a minimum of risk to the equipment," Captain Watts replied, then added as if in afterthought, "provided we keep our axes sharp and our powder dry!"

Nelson looked blankly at the Captain who was perceptive enough to realize that the young man did not grasp his meaning regarding the sharp axes he had mentioned in his previous statement and said, "Mr. Tift, you are aware of the fact that there are no coaling stations along the rivers here in the south and that we have to pull into the banks and tie up now and then, take our axes, go into the forest and replenish our supply of cordwood to keep the boilers going and the steam up?"

Nelson was embarrassed and struggled for an answer. "Why I must have been aware of this burning of wood instead of coal down here! I guess it just did not really register because it has not really concerned the Tift ships up to this point." He paused, then asked, "By the way Captain, when you go ashore to cut the wood are you ever bothered by river ruffians or pirates?"

"Well, the land is very sparsely settled along the Flint, and with the possible exception of the country where the rivers meet we don't really have to worry about checking to see if our powder is dry," the well set set-up, gray-haired captain answered with a laugh.

They talked along for a little while longer, and then Nelson felt that it was the appropriate time to bring up a subject that he had hesitated to broach at the very outset of their conversation. "Captain Watts did we get a good buy in this ship — pardon me, sir, I mean — boat?" Nelson was quick to remember the fine distinction between the terms "boats" and "ships" when seafaring men were concerned.

"Young man, one is never far from a jagged rock, a burst boiler, a big snag, a sand bar, or a blown up engine on these marginally navigable rivers of the southeast United States, and a new steamer will go down as quickly or burn as fast as an old one. I would have to say that the buyers of the 'Mary Emeline' got their money's worth when they purchased her, but she is in need of some engine work when she gets down to Apalachicola." The Captain paused and said, "When the folks in Hawkinsville decided to build this town and get a steamboat I came up-river to Drayton and supervised some of the building of the 'Mary Emeline.' The folks in Drayton were set up to build cotton boxes, small boats and cotton barges. We built much of her there but had to wait several weeks for rain and high water and then poled her down to Apalachicola for the fitting of her boilers, engines and other hardware. It started raining again and we saw precious few people on the way downriver. We had some close calls in the swollen river and I never again want to make such a trip without full steam and control of the wheel."

"We can have the barges and the steamer loaded and ready to go by the day after tomorrow," Nelson said with firm conviction. He looked sideways at Old Hawkins who gave him a barely perceptible nod of his head. Nelson then asked, "Captain Watts, can you tell me how much water the 'Mary Emeline' draws when cargo loaded?"

"She draws three feet and goes to four feet when fully loaded. She is sternwheel self-propelled steam powered; she can carry a crew of sixteen or a crew of eight and eight passengers, and sleep them all. She is one hundred seventy-eight feet overall; hull is one hundred fifty-six feet; her beam is thirty-four feet over-all; her depth is six feet and the draft four feet, loaded. Her displacement is four hundred seventy-one tons loaded; she is fitted with two high pressure joy valve fourteen-inch diameter, seventy-two inch stroke, and her horsepower is one hundred and sixty-seven at twenty RPM per engine. Her boiler is Scotch Marine manufactured in Charleston and has two hundred two pounds of pressure per square inch, one thousand six hundred square feet heating surface. The paddle wheel at the stern is eighteen feet in diameter and twenty feet long; there are fourteen buckets—eighteen feet wide. Now to be perfectly frank with you, son, I don't think we should ever make the run between Hell's Gate and Albany fully loaded unless it is when the high water mark is reached during the rainy season. I believe that we will get much more out of the 'Mary Emeline' if we carry a modest cargo aboard and use her power to move the barges. There are some places even on the Apalachicola River, only fifty miles away from the Bay, where the going can be tough for a fully loaded steamer. We know of places such as Virginia Bend where we sometimes have to go around by utilizing Moccasin Slough, which is crooked, narrow, and badly obstructed with snags and overhanging timbers, and if used, takes several days to negotiate. Nelson, you will be amazed at some of the tricks that we river pilots must employ to get around and over snags, shoals, logs, and sand bars; maneuvers that a sea captain would never stoop to use, but which are the lifeblood of riverboating."

Nelson excused himself to go talk to Hawkins who had gone over to some of the hands who nearly had the barges loaded and ready to go. He found Hawkins talking to the first mate of the "Mary Emeline" and stood with them as they made final plans for getting the "Mary Emeline" loaded.

"I think that we will finish off the barges fust thing in the morning, Nelson, and can get started before noon on the 'Mary Emeline'." He turned to the first mate of the "Mary Emeline" and asked, "Will you be ready for us to start bringing the cargo on by then?"

"Oh, yes, we can be ready by the first thing in the morning if you'd be so inclined," the first mate said in his best-foot-forward manner, obviously wanting to impress the old man and young Tift with his manners as well as the competent handling of his exalted rank.

"First Mate, what is normal running time for your boat under normal conditions to Bainbridge or Fort Gaines, up to Columbus and from there down to the Gulf?" Nelson asked.

"Well, Mr. Tift, let me give you a little background," said the Mate expansively. "Old schooners used to come up into the Flint and the Chattahoochee, and I know an old Captain who brought the 'Fannie' to Bainbridge back in 1827 and to Columbus in 1828. The Masters of the 'Bessie Clary', 'Flint Bride', 'Hard Times', 'Free Trader', and the 'Joke' claim that they intend to make the run on up here to Albany if the traffic will bear such trips. Some say they have already been up here, and others say they turned back at 'Hell's Gate.' But, Mr. Tift, these riverboat men are much like fishermen, and you can't lay too much reliability on what they say when they are bragging about their exploits on the rivers. Now the old 'Virginia' set the record from Apalachicola to Columbus in thirty-eight hours. There are now six steamboats on the regular run between Columbus and the Gulf. Of course, the towns along the flow of the river, like Fort Gaines, Florence or Omaha, Eufaula (Irwintown), Blakely, Franklyn, Shorterville, Abbeville,

Columbia, Sneads, and the towns on down the Apalachicola River also profit from the regular service."

Back aboard the "Mary Emeline" Nelson asked Captain Watts if he thought that the federal government would help with the clearing of the Flint or if he thought that the counties and state would have to bear the expense of keeping the channel clear. "Oh, the counties and states are getting many selected sections of the rivers worked and cleared of snags and sand bars. This tough limestone formation is something else. You consider those solid rock shoals just two hundred yards above here. Why, to remove them will run into real money—much more than a county and maybe even a state could afford. Of course, your immediate problem is between here and Newton, and the biggest one of all is Hell's Gate," Captain Watts replied. "The folks that buy cotton at Bainbridge do not have this problem with their shipping, and they don't have to battle through where the Itchaway-Notchaway comes pouring into the Flint and forms this Hell's Gate, because they load a little below the point where the whirlpool is formed."

"Then it is questionable that they get cargo from this side of the Itchaway-Notchaway? The Bainbridge shippers, I mean."

"Well, Baggs Ferry landing is downriver from where the creeks come into the river. Farmers would have to haul the goods over no-telling-what-kind of roads and get it across the creeks in order to load at Baggs Ferry."

"I see, and how many landings do we pass between here and Bainbridge?"

"Let me see, I was making a rough chart on the way up. Here it is; north of Bainbridge on the east side of the river and not far from Bainbridge port is 'Fairgrounds' then 'Mongs', 'Summerford', 'Humphreys', 'Munroe', 'Swindell', 'Baggs Ferry', 'Newton', 'DeWitt', and 'Albany.' On the west side coming north from Bainbridge are 'Hattons', 'Brutons', 'Free Ferry', 'Donalson', 'Drew Roberts', 'Cox's', 'Baggs Ferry', 'Newton', 'Dewitt', and 'Albany'." The captain paused, lit his stubby little corncob pipe, and continued, "You have the best landing, a warehouse, and a town, but only small cotton boxes can be sent down from above here except in flood time. Who wants to wait and then fight high water in order to get his products downriver and out to the market?"

"Captain Watts, how far is it from Bainbridge to Mount Vernon?"

"Oh, about thirty miles of easy river," the Captain answered and then looked closely at his chart and continued, "Coming upstream from where the rivers meet there is Butlers Creek about fourteen and eight-tenths miles; Faceville Landing is about sixteen and five-tenths miles; Hales Landing is twenty and nine-tenths miles; Four-Mile Creek is twenty-four miles from the junction of the rivers, and then you go around the big horseshoe bend and into the port of Bainbridge. It is one hundred fifty-five miles from the forks of the rivers up to Columbus, but we can get you better acquainted with the rivers once we get underway." The Captain laughed and then said reflectively, "I hope that it will not be too long before big steam dredges come up into the Flint and dig out an eight-foot channel, fifty feet wide, so that the steamboat men will not be plagued with such trials and tribulations as we are experiencing at the present time."

Nelson looked to see if the old Captain was serious about what he had said, and then asked, "Steam-powered dredges to dig out a river channel this far inland? Surely you jest, Captain."

Brother Hawkins had just come back aboard and heard the captain's statement regarding dredging the river and Nelson's subsequent question. He interrupted to ask Nelson, "Did you ever hear of the big steam dredge that was built by Oliver Evans in Philadelphia 'way back before you was born?" The big man paused and winked slyly at Captain Watts.

Now Nelson was certain that the two old men were having fun at his expense, but the Captain spoke up immediately, with the authority of one who knows his facts, "Why, that is absolutely correct, Mr. Hawkins. Oliver Evans built his 'Orkuter Amphibolus' in 1805, and it actually pulled itself slowly down through the streets of Philadelphia."

Nelson looked from one to the other of the old-timers; then full realization hit him that they were perfectly serious. He could not understand how a great achievement in the scientific and nautical fields could have escaped him completely.

"Captain Watts, you just won't believe how smart that boy is about 'most everything under the sun, but every now and again something like this, real important-like, comes along that he never heard tell about," Brother Hawkins explained softly, then added, "I do declare, it do beat all."

Brother Hawkins had engaged an expert in the art of getting unpowered cargo downriver to the Gulf from the Albany area. This man was a Mr. Griffin who had five blacks to whom he had taught all the tricks of the trade and who were rented out for a dollar a day and "found" for the trips to the Gulf. Two of the blacks would be on one of the barges, and two of them would be aboard the other barge with Griffin's lead black who was known as "Red Buck," the latter a highly intelligent, strong riverman who frequently made the trip to the Gulf with his men without the supervision of Mr. Giffin or anyone else. Captain Watts told Nelson that Hawkins had made a shrewd selection of men to take care of the barges; Griffin and his men had a fine reputation with the river people. "They are real river roustabouts and, like all keelboat men, are strong and fun-loving, but they are also very honest and loyal," explained Captain Watts.

Nelson was determined to make the trip so that he could gain experience on the river and with the steamboat. He wanted to be there to supervise the loading of the large cargo his brothers had shipped to Apalachicola for him. He also wanted to make contacts with prospective customers on the way downriver and to purchase a wide variety of supplies needed by his customers in the Albany area—supplies not normally available through his usual sources of supply at Key West or Charleston. The big items that he needed to find were two steam-driven sawmills, one heavy and one light. One was to be designed more or less for stationary installation, and the other one, not too heavy, was to be placed aboard a floating mill that he and Hawkins had constructed, so that it could be floated to the timber rather than the timber floated to the mill.

"Brother Hawkins, you will be in complete charge until I get back from the Gulf. Now I know, as you say, you feel a little 'put-out and spat-on' not being able to go with me, but someone has to stay and be in charge of the town. I have sent a letter to Charles asking him to make plans to break off what he is doing in Hawkinsvile and come on down here. When he gets here, you and I can move around a little more freely, meet all the people here in southwest Georgia, and get to know ever person and trail in it."

"Well, Nelson, I'll tell a man that I'll be mighty proud when Charles does get here and all that comes to pass. Heck, I don't know nothing about buying and selling land, and it'd scare the pants off me if somebody allowed as how he would be obliged if I'd sell him a parcel of land. Now I'll build him a house or a store, or even put him up a mill, but I just don't know nothing about all this kind of business stuff and all."

"All you have to do is tell a prospective customer that you will take the necessary message for me and that you think that it will be all right for him to see this card that explains about the prices of lots and how they will be paid for," Nelson said as he handed the unhappy oldster the information.

"Nelson, I know you got lots on yer mind, but I want to tell you afore you go down to Florida that I been thinking about taking another trip to Argyle to kinda look around and visit a spell. I hate to think that I might come down with the fever or something and be a burden on you in my old age and my infirmities. If I get to feeling low, I better get on back to Argyle anyways, as a man oughta be laid to rest in his native soil." It was the first time that Hawkins had ever hinted of death or advancing old age in the period of more than a decade that Nelson had known him. He could see that the faithful old fellow was genuinely embarrassed by admitting that old age was creeping up on him.

Nelson put his arm around his old friend and said, "Charles should be here in a few days, and after you have shown him around and explained to him the way we conduct business at the store and the warehouse, the shipping and buying of cotton and the selling of town lots, I think you should catch the stage to Savannah and have your visit with your folks at Argyle. I know we have both been pushing too hard, and I am prone to forget sometimes about the difference in our ages. I know if I am worn out at the end of the day how very bad you must feel; but look around us and see what we have accomplished."

Brother Hawkins turned and looked down Front Street where several new buildings stood. On Broad there were several structures above what they considered the high-water mark, but each located so as to get close to the Broad Street landing. All of these marks of progress, along with the big warehouse and a small number of new frame buildings on Washington, Pine, and Jackson Streets comprised the business section of Albany. A score of dwellings had been built and several other houses were under construction. The old man turned and said, "Nelson, I'm aggona take you up on that stage ride, soon's Charles gets here, and I shows him around a mite. I aim to be back though, afore them steam engines come so I can set them up the way they's 'sposed to be."

"Brother Hawkins, what do you think about buying a few slaves to help with the labor around here?" Nelson asked. He wanted to feel Hawkins out on this subject that had always been a little, if not very controversial to both of them.

"Now you done asked me, and so I'll tell ye straight," the old man shot back at the younger man. He continued in more conciliatory tone, "Boy, you know my feelings concerning the blacks and any other color of man so long's he's a child of the Almighty. You don't need no slaves of yo' own when ye can rent 'em so cheap, and you knows the woods is full of 'Fadeaways,' passing theyselves off as mulattoes who is willing and able to do a day's work now and again for stuff you can let 'em have from the store. Nelson, this is your town, and you ought to call the shots when it comes to downright mistreatement of bonded folk and slaves. I would say offer a fair price to the man who mistreats the unfortunates under him, and if he don't take what you offer, then run him out of yore town. If we gets folks like these unwanted and beaten creatures, I says that it would be our Christian duty to buy or take them, use them, and give them a decent home."

"It shall be as you say, Brother Hawkins." Nelson then asked, "Did you mean the Indians who did not go west with the army when you referred to the 'Fadaways'?"

"Yep, the same ones that old Winfield Scott just kinda left laying around out in the swamps that did not want to go with the army."

Nelson thought a moment and then said, "You know, I have noticed a marked difference between the blacks of Charleston and Augusta and these over here in this territory.

You say that some of the blacks that we rent from the 'owners' are either all or part Creek Indians?"

"Just like you said in yore letter to Asa and Amos, the folks hereabouts do talk to me a heap easier then they does to you," the old man laughed.

"Have you heard anything about the folks over around Kinnard's Landing on the Kinchafoonee Creek?"

"Shore! One of the carpenters told me right off about the 'blacks' working around Albany and how lots of them are from around Kinnard's Landing. They have a big, well-educated half-breed who is their leader. He has white friends who 'rent' these 'blacks' for him, as their bonafide slaves."

"Well, I did suspect this was going on, and one does live and learn," Nelson said as he continued to get his personal gear together to take aboard the "Mary Emeline." At last they were ready. At least half of the adult population of Baker County plus many of their children were at the landing to see the "Mary Emeline" start upstream from the landing and then turn in a graceful half circle to point her bow downstream. Captain Watts watched Nelson out of the corner of his eye and noted the anxious look on the young pioneer's face. "Fear naught, Nelson. The mate checked out the 'turn-around' yesterday, and Albany has one of the best I have ever seen." Nelson heaved a sigh of relief as this had been a secret dread that had bothered him regarding whether they did have a good 'turn-around' for boats at the head of navigation. He relaxed and watched the complicated procedure as the "Mary Emeline" eased up to the waiting barges and nosed into them. The necessary attachments were made, and the steamboat pushed them easily out into the river. They were on their way to the Gulf of Mexico. The old Captain, still watching the young man out of the corner of his eye, saw Nelson's lips move in a silent prayer for their safe voyage.

Captain Watts blew the big steam whistle as he neared each landing, and crowds of people flocked to each place to yell and wave their arms. Nelson had resolved to work on his journal, which he had sadly neglected lately. He could not keep his mind on writing in his diary as there were just too many things to see and things happening all around him, so he put it away until another day. The captain kept showing his large submerged logs and snags, bends in the river, sandbars, and rock formations. Nelson knew that he must watch the charts, listen to the captain and the first mate, and study the navigation of the river. Captain Watts turned the big wooden wheel over to him several times so that he could get the "feel" of the stern-wheeler. He resolved to put his full powers of concentration into learning everything he could about the river and riverboat navigation, the people along the river, and the merchants at the ports and landings from Albany to the Gulf of Mexico.

The "Mary Emeline" tied up at Newton, the county seat of Baker County, which had been moved from Byron several years before. Newton was a village that had been named for John Newton, a Revolutionary soldier. The courthouse was a frame building sitting off the side of the sandy road less than an eighth of a mile from the landing. Several stores clustered around the courthouse. There were two taverns, one of which had rooms to let, and Nelson noted two big boarding houses on the other side of the road with a score or more of houses in the general vicinity.

Several men were resting on their haunches by the front steps of the courthouse and spoke to Nelson as he started inside. He came back down the steps and introduced himself to each man. When they found out who he was, one of them laughingly said, "Mr. Tift, the clerk of the Superior and the Inferior courts, Mr. Thomas F. Whittington, is really going to be happy to see you, and as far as that goes, so is Sheriff Stafford Long and our surveyor, Mr. Jonathon C. Neil." Nelson smiled and had a good laugh with the "courthouse crowd" and went inside. There were two rooms on each side of the dark, cramped hallway. One door, standing slightly open, was neatly lettered, "Clerk." He gave it a courteous knock and went inside.

"Good day, Sir. I am Nelson Tift from Albany, and I have some business to transact with you," Nelson stated to the man who sat at a rough document-cluttered desk. Thomas Whittington was an intelligent-appearing man about Nelson's age. He looked up from the mass of papers before him with a smile of relief on his face, got up from the desk, and came around to introduce himself and to shake Nelson's outstretched hand.

"Well, as I live and breathe! There is such a man after all. It is about time — those partners of yours from Hawkinsville have forwarded every conceivable sort of instrument dealing with land transactions down here on nearly every stage that drops the mail for us just across the river. The ones from you folks in Albany I have been able to get registered all right, but you will have to sit down with me and the Sheriff and Mr. Neil, our county surveyor. The coronor, John Gillion, wants to see you about some lost or misplaced deeds that have to do with the Albany area." The clerk noted the surprised look on Nelson's face and hurried to explain, "No, I don't want to infer that the coronor has anything to do with my office; it is just that when the records were being moved from Byron to Newton this courthouse was not quite ready, and Mr. Gillion kept them for a few days at his place in Gillionville. Somewhere along the line, the papers got misplaced."

"Mr. Whittington, I will be happy to sit down with you and help get this administrative work cleared up. You know we simply must do something about the condition of the road from Albany to Newton and have a bridge or two built. We just cannot get back and forth in bad weather; even a man and horse have a rough time of it in ideal weather," Nelson said as they slowly worked their way through the red tape of validating and recording the deeds and other documents. Nelson saw that his partners in Hawkinsville had indeed been busy, as there was everything from simple quit-claim deeds to the sale of plantations to be cleared up and the transactions duly recorded. Many of the deals involved Alexander Shotwell, either as the buyer or the seller. Nelson remarked to the clerk that he knew the man.

"Mr. Tift, I sure would appreciate it if you could get word to Shotwell that it is imperative that he get down here and see me at his earliest convenience. Many things are at a standstill at this office due to the lack of proper signatures, unpaid fees and the general lack of information in regard to some of these land deals. If you can get word to him on these things, tell him that the sheriff and surveyor also want to see him," the man implored. Nelson assured the clerk that he would get word to Alexander Shotwell, and they continued working their way through the documents, each helping the other with needed information, until they had finished. Nelson knew that he simply had to get his daily journal and make notations of all these transactions as he was already so far behind that he might never catch up. He now became acutely aware that the Hawkinsville partners had made many sales of which he had no record and that there was now a possibility that he, without meaning to, would sell the same piece of property that someone at another site had already purchased from his partners.

The word had gotten around quickly about the steamer and the two barges being at the Newton landing. Nelson picked up over fifty bales of cotton which were distributed between the boat and the barges to be taken for local farmers to the warehouses in Bainbridge. Nelson invited officials at the courthouse to accompany him down to the landing and go aboard the "Mary Emeline" to met the Captain. Nelson learned during the ensuing conversation that the "Viola" had been up as far as Newton the week before and had delivered a sawmill from St. Joseph, Florida. The Captain of the "Viola" had asked about the new town of Albany, but when some of the "boys" down at the landing remarked that boats as big as the "Viola" did not dare go any farther upstream, the "Viola" turned and went back to Bainbridge.

Nelson turned to Captain Watts and asked, "Do we have any paint and paint brushes aboard?" The Captain nodded his head in the affirmative and sent for the desired items. When a "hand" returned to them, Nelson lowered himself into the dinghy and painted a foot-high outline of the words "Albany, Georgia," underneath the boat's nameplate on the starboard and then came over and did the same on the landing side. He then went back on board and told the Captain to have one of the crew fill in the outlined letters with black paint, saying, "Now every boat captain that sees the "Mary Emeline" will know that Albany, Georgia is the head of navigation on the Flint River."

Nelson's new friends went ashore, and the steamboat eased on downriver. Tension began to mount about eight miles downstream, and the Captain told Nelson, "We are approaching 'Hell's Gate', and here it will pay off to have such men as those of Captain Griffin's and his crew in charge of the barges. If things go wrong, those big barges could take this ship and perhaps some of us to a certain death. Try to keep your eyes glued on the barges instead of the enormous current that comes into this river here and causes what we call 'Hell's Gate'. If things do go wrong, Griffin and his men will use their sharp axes to quickly cut loose from the "Mary Emeline" and try to take the barges through by sheer guts, strength, and experience."

"What happens after the barges get through the big whirlpool?" Nelson asked.

"The barges will possibly be whirled around a few times and thrown clear back into the channel and calmer waters, and we will in that case pick them back up and continue downstream. At worst, one or both of them might be thrown up on a shoal where we can either work them off or wait for a little high water and float them off," the Captain said, shrugging his shoulders as he voiced their options.

"Why, Captain, if one of those barges does go up on the shoals, and we can't work it off, we might be waiting here for days — even weeks — for the water to rise enough to float them off," Nelson wailed in youthful frustration.

"On, no, this happens quite often with both cotton boxes and barges," the Captain answered. "The 'Mary Emeline' will continue on downstream, and the men on the barge will wait and work themselves off the shoal and drift downstream. They are experts at this sort of thing and are prepared for the hazards of their trade." Nelson turned and waved to Mr. Griffin, and that hardy individual gave him back the "all's well" sign used by seamen and riverboat men the world over.

Nelson resolved to settle down and learn everything he possibly could from this experience. The river in front of them broadened perceptibly as the brown torrent of the Itchaway-Notchaway Creek — which was really a river itself by the time it had been joined by the Pachitla, Chickasawhatchee, and many lesser creeks and branches — came pouring into the Flint. Not only was this stream pouring into the Flint; it was challenging the river. This challenge by the Notchaway being met by the answer to that challenge by the mighty Flint was what caused the unbelievable whirlpool that now lay directly in their path.

"Pull the whistle! I want them to cut loose now!" yelled the Captain to his first mate. The whistle shrieked, and the sharp axes of the keelboat men came down at the same moment. The great shuddering strength that had suddenly gripped the "Mary Emeline" was suddenly gone as the ropes holding her to the big barges were severed. The Captain had the stern paddlewheel reversed, and he pulled back from the edge of the powerful whirlpool and stood close in to shore where they watched helplessly as the barges went down into the crazy, swirling, jumping whirlpool. Now Nelson knew why men spoke of "Hell's Gate" with fear and near-reverence. Those on the deck of the "Mary Emeline" felt like a family of people watching a child taking its first few steps and being helpless to move and catch it when it stumbled and fell. The first barge with "Red Buck" in charge was flung around once and into Notchaway Creek, which promptly spat it back into the river with such force that it broke through the mighty centrifugal pull of the whirlpool and continued its course down the river where the blacks maneuvered it into shore on the western bank to await the "Mary Emeline."

The second barge, with Griffin in charge, was not so fortunate when it was drawn down into the vortex of the whirlpool. It made three revolutions, getting farther out from the "eye" each time it went around until it was suddenly flung out of the whirlpool and onto a dreaded sandbar where it sat—high and dry! "Looks like the men are all right, and the barge is not harmed, but she sure looks like she will have to be floated off. Now everybody get ready to make the run ourselves." The Captain pulled slowly away from the shore and aimed the "Mary Emeline" directly at the center of the whirlpool at full speed ahead. Nelson thought for one moment that he was back at sea in a wild storm as there was a sudden drop of the "Mary Emeline" and then the great and powerful paddle wheel at the stern bit into the water of the giant whirlpool and shot them across the maw of the wildly swirling water. The blunt bow of the "Mary Emeline" bit into the other side of the maelstrom and tore through it and to freedom from it. Every man on board cheered lustily as they shot out of the mouth of Hell's Gate. The Captain eased the "Mary Emeline" over to a landing on the west side of the river next to the ferry. They took a path back upriver a hundred yards or so and went out onto the sand where Griffin and his men were stranded aboard their barge. Nelson and the Captain found the men in good spirits as men usually are after an exciting adventure from which they have emerged unscathed. "What do you think, Mr. Griffin? Will she have to wait for high water?" Captain Watts asked.

"Yes, Sir, Cap'n! There's not enough power in southwest Georgia to pull this weight off this sandpit. But it will more than likely be raining next week. Me and my crew will go back downriver in our little lifeboat, and 'Red Buck' and his boys will come up from here and swap with us." Griffin paused and then said, "Mr. Tift, we have off-loaded the bales of cotton in other cases like this, and it has helped float the barges and cotton boxes off with just a little rise in the river. I know where I can get several cotton boxes near here and have the men who are going to stay here anyway start loading from the barge into those boxes."

Nelson looked quickly at Captain Watts to see what his reaction to this suggestion might be. "That's right, Nelson, and it will sure work. I say we should have the men go ahead and do it," Captain Watts said quickly.

Nelson turned to Mr. Griffin and said, "We will certainly appreciate it if you will put your plan into action, Sir."

The "Mary Emeline" proceeded to Bainbridge without further incident. Nelson was at the wheel, and the river was comparatively easy to navigate, as it was broad, not overly swift, and free of impediments. They tied up at the foot of Jackson Street, and Nelson went ashore. The roustabouts started unloading the cotton and other cargo which was invoiced Bainbridge. Nelson found this southwest Georgia town much further advanced than Albany. It was the county seat of Decatur County and had been incorporated in 1829. Nelson remembered reading a paper called *The Southern Spy* that had been printed in Bainbridge in 1829, which said that there were one hundred and forty inhabitants, some of whom had been living there for five years, and not one grave had been dug during that time, nor was there a sick person in town.

Nelson walked up to Lester's Boarding House and met Mr. F. G. Arnett who introduced himself and took Nelson over to his store and showed him around the little "square." "Mr. Tift, Decatur County was formed out of Early County in 1823 and our first county officers were John Gray as sheriff; Jacob Harrell as cornor; B. B. Douglas, surveyor; and Daniel O'Neel, clerk of Superior Court. This little 'square' where we are standing used to be part of 'El Camino Real' or as folks hereabouts say 'The King's Highway'. It was first an Indian trail which connected St. Augustine with Pensacola during the Spanish rule in these parts. Farther west it became known as the Mission Trail because the Spanish had built a string of missions all the way from St. Augustine to San Diego on the Pacific Ocean. The 'Real' crossed the Flint here at the trading post of old James Burgess. There have been many battles fought in this vicinity between the Indians and the Spanish, the English and the Spanish, and more recently, between Andrew Jackson and the Seminoles. Old Fort Hughes, Scott, the Negro Fort and Camp Recovery, are all near here." Arnett paused for breath and then added, "There has been some form of civilization here since DeSoto discovered the Flint River, which he called the Capachequi. DeSoto built barges here in 1540 to float his troops and their equipment across the river."

Nelson remembered the story that old Hawkins had told him about Fort Scott and the Creek Chief Menewa who had been in charge of it during Jackson's probe into Florida after the wily Seminoles. Nelson then asked, "When Andrew Jackson was at Fort Scott in 1818, did he leave some men under the Upper Creek War Chief, Menewa?"

"Well, I'll be darned. How did you know about that?" Mr. Arnett asked in surprise.

"I have an old friend who was with Jackson and Chief Menewa," Nelson answered with a certain amount of pride.

"Well, lemme see . . . they abandoned the fort in 1821, but it is still some distance south of here near Hutchinson's Ferry, if you'd be of a mind to see it," Arnett said, and then added as an afterthought, "Yes, Sir, General Jackson arrived here with his staff and troops from the Georgia Militia. He was joined by woodsmen from Kentucky and his old Tennessee mountain boys, who had marched down through Alabama, into Georgia, and on down along the east side of the Chattahoochee on the Three Notch Trail. Jackson consolidated his troops here and left Chief Menewa with sixty men to hold the fort and the forks of the rivers until he could conquer the rest of the

Seminoles and the Spanish, as well as some English malcontents who were causing unrest in the panhandle of western Florida and up into the rivers of southwest Georgia and southeast Alabama."

"Do you have the only general store in town?" asked Nelson after they had talked a little about the weather, about local, state, and national politics, and the state of the economy.

"Oh, no, I hope that I have not led you to believe so. Peabody and Company have a very active store. We have three doctors: Holt, Saunders, and Bruce. There are two lawyers: Goulden and Barry. We have a Methodist church and a circuit rider who comes through every other Sunday. There are two active carpenters in town. Our little courthouse is occupied mostly by Lester's goat, and there ain't no door on it. We have a little jail, such as it is, with the same affliction regarding the doors, but it don't really need a door as we got no prisoners. Now Mr. Shows, who also makes breeches and coats for the naked, is our Justice of the Peace. Jerry Taylor is our blacksmith and constable. We have a cake shop run by old Rachel, who also runs a Saturday night dance home for the colored ladies and such. There is two gin houses with very little in them, if you know what I mean, and whiskey is sold by Lovick Moore, and by Peabody and Company. Old Sam is their chief patron. He sells watermelons and fish to pay for his whiskey. We have two young, very pretty ladies who teach at what we call the Academy. Dr. Baker is the headmaster (he is sober part of the time and has ten students) and, oh, yes, we have a washerwoman who picks up and delivers folks' clothes at the boarding house."

"Well, I would say that you people have a fine start for a booming city here at Bainbridge. Mr. Arnett, I am going to try to do business with as many people as I can here in your town. Would you be kind enough to give me some of the names of the families around here?"

"Why, most of a certainty, Mr. Tift. First, if I may be so bold as to inquire, what kind of business you intend to transact with these people?" asked the now suddenly-very-practical Mr. Arnett.

"Well, as you might know, I have a very strong tie-in with wholesale merchants in Hawkinsville, Augusta, and even

Charleston. I also have brothers in the wholesale business at Key West, Florida, who can ship across to Apalachicola and up here to Bainbridge at a considerable reduction in cost to all concerned."

"Now you are speaking my language, Mr. Tift. Pray continue, Sir."

"Well, to show my good intentions to begin with, I will let you have some of the items that will be waiting on the docks for me at Apalachicola when we get down there this trip," Nelson offered.

"Very good, friend Tift. It has been hard here to reach out to the outside world and find a real contact, one that would be around to go back on if something proved unsatisfactory. Now, about the families hereabouts. There are Thomas Biship, George Barry, Dr. Saunders, Dr. Bruce, the O'Neels. We count Alexander Shotwell, as he has much land hereabouts, although he stays on the stage 'tween here and Macon most of the time. Now, Mr. Tift, most of us around here come from poor, fearless, tough, homes, but unlettered Scotch-Irish immigrants. The ox and wagon is our standard method of travel and power when not using the river. Horseback is first class and buggies are for only the very high-placed. Daniel Odom Neel picked this spot out for the town to be built. He chose it because of high ground, a good, deep landing on the river, and being near where old Burgess had his trading post on the Indian trail. They had a mite of trouble locating the person who had 'drawn' the land but located him in Fleming's District, Florida. He was William Harper and was satisfied to sell lot number two hundred twenty-two in the fifteenth land district to the founders of Bainbridge for twenty dollars, 'in hand to him paid,' all two hundred fifty acres of it. Old Burgess had died in 1799, but a few of his descendents are still hereabouts, as are some of the 'Bully's', as far as that goes." Arnett paused to think a moment and reflect.

"Who is the Bully?" Nelson asked, taking advantage of the pause in conversation, but not really wanting to interrupt the train of thought of this backwoods historian, as he found Mr. Arnett's chronicle of the little town's past very fascinating.

"Oh, the Bully?" Arnett laughed, "Well, 'The Bully' ran this country for William Augustus Bowles and was a 'holy terror.' He was Spanish, and said to be a descendent of the great and gentle Cumbrian Giant, Velascola. Velascola was the Spanish priest who was beloved by the Indians at St. Simons Island, but who was tomahawked to death in 1587 when they found out that he had fathered a child of their chief's daughter. The girl and her son were banished far to the west to where the Chattahoochee and the Flint Rivers form the Apalachicola. 'The Bully" had three daughters born of his three wives; there was never a son, and when 'the Bully' died in 1790, the daughters married runaway slaves and Indians. Their descendents are still in these parts." Arnett ended the little story and added, "You were asking about the families before I got off on another story. We had the families of William Chester, Duncan Cury, James Bell, Peter Douglas, Patrick Sessions, Anthony Hutchins, Solomon Belton, Reuben Cloud, James Brown, James W. Fanning, and Marcellous Smith. It is hard to believe that all of the land owned by these families used to be a royal grant from Spain to 'the Bully' and later to the Panton and Leslie Trading Company and the lower Creek Indians, but of course, as you know, Horseshoe Bend and the Jackson treaty ended all that."

"How much shipping do you have out of your fine port here, Mr. Arnett?" Nelson asked casually.

"Lemme see, I think that Marcellous Smith, the publisher of our *Southern Spy*, said that we shipped five thousand bales of cotton down to Apalachicola in 1830, and it has been picking up each year since then. We have the 'Planter', 'Southern', 'Columbus', 'Anna Calhoun', 'Metamora', 'Arab', 'Georgiana', 'Ohioan', 'Native Georgian', 'Versailles', and the 'Viola' making regular runs to Columbus and the Bay from here. We have the Florida mail line which leaves Mobile every other day by coastal steamer to Pensacola and Cedar Bluff. From there four horse coaches bring the mail via Marianna, Mount Vernon, here, Pindertown, Hawkinsville, Sandersville, Louisville, and Augusta. They connect with the Charleston Railroad and steam packets for Norfolk, Philadelphia, Baltimore, New York, Staten Island, New London, and Boston," said Arnett proudly.

"My goodness, Mr. Arnett, you are certainly well-informed about river, mail and stage traffic, as well as the history of these parts."

"Well, as a public servant, I feel it is my duty to be well-informed."

"Oh, I was not aware that you also held public office, Mr. Arnett!"

"Oh, yes, I have recently been appointed to a commission, along with Mr. Thomas Hines and Mr. Donalson, to improve navigation from Bainbridge to the Old Creek Agency in Crawford County which is, as you no doubt know, away above your town of Albany. We aim to do as much for the roads and the river as Bennett Crawford and his three cohorts, who were appointed by the 1827 legislature, accomplished. We have come a long way since the days before the 'Fanny'—owned by Blake and Ingersoll—came to Bainbridge back in 1827. They used pole barges and boats here before the coming of the 'Fanny'," Arnett said with some show of enthusiasm.

Nelson thanked Arnett for giving him so much of his time and indicated that he had better be getting back to the landing as the steamer must be ready to depart by now. Mr. Arnett invited him to Uncle Billy Malone's "Buzzard Roost" for a drink, and when Nelson declined his offer, Arnett said, "You must have heard it is a rough place. There have been some shady things happening there and some real funny ones—like the time (back three or four years) when Owen O'Neel challenged Dan Odom Neel to a duel over old Dan's pretty daughter, who Owen O'Neel wanted to marry," Arnett laughed as he remembered the spirited exchange of choice expletives used by the principles of the altercation.

"Well, for goodness sakes, Mr. Arnett, what happened? Did they fight?"

"Naw, they never left the bar until they left arm in arm late that night. Of course, the young man married old Dan's daughter, and they are one of our best families," Arnett laughed.

Captain Watts was all set to resume the voyage to Apalachicola when Nelson arrived at the landing where the "Mary Emeline" was tied up. Steam was up, and they cast off. It was smooth-going downstream, and Nelson handled the "Mary Emeline" all the way to the spot where beautiful Spring Creek and the mighty Chattahoochee met the Flint and formed the Apalachicola. Captain Watts, who had been at Nelson's elbow since leaving Bainbridge, took the wheel and showed

Nelson exactly how to steer into the Apalachicola. They tied up for the night at Mount Vernon, Florida, within two hundred yards of where Andrew Jackson and his army of the Southwest had crossed on their way to the Battle of New Orleans. The Captain and most of his crew went ashore to visit the taverns of the riverboat town. Mr. Griffin stayed aboard the barge with his men, and Nelson, by lamp light, took advantage of the opportunity to bring his journal up to date and to chart what he could remember of the voyage to this point.

Chapter 4

The voyage down the Apalachicola had been interesting, enlightening, and uneventful. The river was wide but low in several places. Nelson charted these trouble spots in his journal and listened attentively to Captain Watts as he skillfully piloted the "Mary Emeline" through Moccasin Slough and other short cuts and detours. The shoreline had changed from limestone to sand and now to tropical mangroves that covered the banks and even grew out into the water. The Apalachicola was now miles wide in places and getting wider as they neared the bay area. More and more boats were in evidence filling the river with motion; some were going across, some upstream, and some were coming into the Apalachicola from adjoining sloughs and creeks and following the same general channel as the "Mary Emeline." Sea gulls, pelicans, and a myriad of other water-fowl wheeled around the steamer and the barge. The musty smell of the river had given away to the salty smell of the Gulf of Mexico. The wind had quickened, and the water was now quite choppy in comparison with that of the inland river.

The "Mary Emeline" nosed the barge into a position alongside the docks where it was pulled in close and secured. The Captain then backed off, came into a nearby wharf, and secured their craft. After they had tied up, the men went ashore into Apalachicola. Warehouses and wharves were all built of the same sturdy material salvaged from cotton boxes that had been floated down from Georgia and Alabama for years.

Nelson located the warehouse to which the cotton was billed and the one to which his shipment from Key West had been forwarded. He then went into the town and opened his financial transactions with a draft on Boyce and Company of Charleston in favor of Raymond and Allison payable in seventy-five days for three thousand dollars. He also drew one to Rawls,

King and Company in favor of the same, due sixty days after date for two thousand dollars. Nelson then gave a Rawls-Tift note in favor of Raymond and Allison for two thousand five hundred dollars payable not more than twelve days after 21 January. Nelson knew that he had better get to Hawkinsville as soon as possible and cover this one. The Apalachicola bank refused to discount over five thousand dollars of any transaction so he insured the shipment for more than five thousand dollars and left the papers with Allison and Raymond. He also left them a draft on Boyce and Company for two thousand five hundred dollars for the purpose of raising money to meet the Tift-Rawls note if necessary.

Several of his new business associates took him to a dinner where the new Trinity Episcopal Church was being organized by Mr. George Field, Colin Mitchell, John Gorrie, E. Wood, George Middlebrook, Hiram Nourse, William G. Porter, E. Bartlett, and L. S. Chittenden. Nelson was introduced to the famous Apalachicola Bay oysters. He found them absolutely delicious, both on the half-shell and fried. He was told that they also made a delicious stew from the oysters. Of course, the young businessman was quick to perceive that here was a commodity that, if it could be transported to Albany without shrinkage or spoilage, would go a long way toward bringing in trade that might otherwise go to other towns. He sent a letter to Asa to arrange for shipment of ice to John Gorrie who expressed interest in the project and agreed to ship oysters to Albany, in season, when the ice came from Key West. Captain Watts accepted the change in plans without the bat of an eye when Nelson explained about the urgency of his traveling to St. Joseph to see about his steam sawmills and the necessity of his getting back to Hawkinsville quickly. He could not afford the delay if he went with them on the "Mary Emeline," which was scheduled to go to Columbus and then stop back by Fort Gaines and Bainbridge before proceeding to Albany. Captain Watts had planned to stop for a few days at Fort Gaines, which was the home port for many of the steamer's crew as well as the home of the Captain himself. They could get some needed repairs done to the "Mary Emeline" during daylight hours and visit with their families and friends after dark. Nelson stood at the docks and saw the trim little steamboat puff off upstream on its return trip into Georgia. All of his shipment had been loaded and was bound for the new town of Albany.

Preliminary arrangements were made between Nelson and the Wood Supply Company of St. Joseph. He had found that the firm had a branch office in Apalachicola and had been shown two models of exactly what he needed. The order was placed; the salesman did not know exactly how much they would cost and the shipping costs and other minor details, but they were able to agree to the general cost. Nelson left fifty dollars with the agent to "bind" the deal.

"You just crate the engines and all component parts and have them placed on the wharf. Send the bill of lading on to me, and I will come or send my steamer to pick them up. Make the terms of payment whatever is usual for your company in similar transactions. You may also tell your people that I would be delighted to act as their agent up in the new country of southwest Georgia at the town of Albany, which is at the head of navigation for the Flint River. I should be able to place quite a number of orders up there for their mills and mill parts from my store. There would be no problems of transporation, as my company owns its own steamboat and could carry the mills that I would sell for them far up the Flint and all the way to Columbus on the Chattahoochee. Tell them that I believe that the venture should prove most beneficial to all parties concerned."

On the twenty-first of January, 1837, Nelson left Apalachicola on his way to Hawkinsville. He took the steamer "Chamoise" to Mount Vernon where he paid the boat Captain ten dollars for his passage. He was most fortunate to be in time for the stage and for having a Mr. Davis of Mount Vernon as a fellow passenger. Brother Davis, lately of Liberty County, told Nelson many tales about the three rivers area. He arrived in Hawkinsville on 24 January, 1837, and hastened to see Squire John Rawls at the bank. Rawls told him in no uncertain terms that his purchases at Apalachicola would not be approved by Rawls and King Company and that they further refused to raise any money in any way except by individual contribution by the several partners on a proportioned basis. The draft made by Nelson at Apalachicola was discounted, and Nelson returned to Albany—empty handed, heavy of heart, and troubled by his partners' lack of support.

Charles was waiting for him in Albany with more bad news. The large barge was still stranded on the shoal below Newton, and the "Mary Emeline" was stuck on Reaton's Shoal with the other barge. Nelson took a canoe and one strong paddler and headed downstream for Reaton's Shoal to see what could be done. He found the steamer fast aground and all the hands off the job and frolicking around with the people of the area. Captain Watts had gone looking for help and while the cat was away the mice were determined to play and refused to work for the First Mate, who had been left in charge. Nelson had been down this road before. He fired several of the ring leaders on the spot and told them, "I give you my word that you will not be tolerated in the town of Albany. Now I want you off this boat and these barges within the hour, or I will see that you are horsewhipped for this disgraceful conduct. As for the rest of you, I care not whether you stay or go and you are free to leave now, but I do promise you that if you stay with me, you will regret that you did not leave with the others unless you are prepared to work, and to work hard, to get these vessels floating again. Now, you three," and Nelson brandished his walking cane at the malcontents, "get out of here and out of my sight before I cane you!"

The re-animated hands went to work with a vengeance. Captain Watts returned with the small barge that ran between Bainbridge and Pindertown; he had borrowed it for the emergency, and they off-loaded cotton from the grounded barge and cargo from the steamer. After one back-breaking week of hard work, they succeeded in getting a barge and the steamer to Albany and the other barge on its way to the Gulf of Mexico. They found Rawls and King awaiting their arrival at the landing at the foot of Broad Street, all ready to close out Tift accounts. They proposed to take cost and be released from all responsibility. Nelson was caught in the middle and was forced to accept their terms since he had signed pledges and documents on both ends. Robert Taylor was reluctant to burden this young man and tried to make it as easy as possible for him when Nelson took over the Taylor interest along with the rest. Hiram Atkerson furnished six thousand dollars and Nelson raised another one thousand dollars which total was applied to the debts of the company for the goods. The debt was due prior to the first of December, 1838, as well as all other debts and goods previously obligated.

Brother Hawkins exploded when he found out what had happened at the "show-down" of Rawls-King, Rawls-Tift, and all the others involved in the big break-up of the Albany Trading Company. "Why, it plain ain't fair to burden a boy like you with all these debts. Son, you could go to prison for defaulting on all this property and all these outstanding obligations they have saddled you with. Why don't you tell them to take it all, and we will go back to Key West where Asa really wants and needs us now that Amos is sure to leave there for good?"

Nelson laughed bitterly at the old-timer's solution to the whole thing. He knew that the old man was loyal to him and angry because he was getting the short end of the stick from these experienced businessmen. He tried to calm Hawkins down by telling him, "Brother Hawkins, I thought I made some good sound investments for my partners. I just don't know why they have flown off the handle so quickly and are so anxious to dump the whole thing in my lap unless they have knowledge of a serious financial situation that is soon to confront the United States. Be that as it may, there is a real chance, barring a serious financial panic, that we can work ourselves out of this mess and emerge from this tangle of misfortune and debt victorious and sitting on top of the world!"

"And how in tarnation will ye be doing that, me fine boy?" Old Hawkins snorted in disbelief.

"You know, Nelson might be right," interposed Charles who had just come over from the landing. "We can turn this whole thing around if we work hard and use our heads. We have transportation, plenty of merchandise to sell on a retail basis to individuals and on wholesale basis to retail merchants in this area. We are going to have two steam-powered sawmills here in a week or so, and we can get plenty of supplies from Key West at prices far below what the other wholesalers and retailers of this area have to pay. Most of all, we have town lots to sell and plenty of farm land and timber."

Nelson immediately took heart, as did Brother Hawkins. What Charles had just said gave them both the motivation they needed to fight back. "By golly, we'll do 'er," shouted Nelson and turned to Brother Hawkins to say, "You go ahead and catch a stage over to Argyle and have your visit out. By the time you get back here we will be well on our way to digging out of this financial trap." He then turned to Charles and continued, "Now here is what we have done: we have given Atkerson one-ninth of the whole business, and we are ready to sell to T. C. McClay of St. Joseph a one-ninth part of three lots of land that Albany is being built on. McClay is going to pay us two thousand dollars for the three lots and we will be receiving from day to day payments on town lots being sold. I am leaving for Macon and Augusta in the morning to make further arrangements. While on this trip, I will buy and sell land to our advantage."

While in Augusta, Nelson proceeded to look up some of his old friends and was laughingly told by them that they had heard he owned about half of southwest Georgia and was doing really well down there. "Well, hardly," Nelson laughed, "but I am trying to pay for a big portion of it."

"Seriously, Nelson, we do know some parties who might be interested in southwest Georgia property, so why don't we go over to the Planter's Hotel and discuss the situation at length?" said John Hatfield. Before the night was over, Nelson had sold four-eighteenths of the same lots he had sold portions of before leaving Albany; these sales were conditional and at the same rate as the others. One prospective buyer said he had three lots of land in Baker County that he would sell for five hundred dollars on the basis of one-half cash and the balance due the first of January, 1838.

"I'll take that land, sight unseen," said Nelson, and he paid the man two hundred fifty dollars in cash while John Hatfield signed the note on the balance as endorser. Nelson left Augusta by stage the following morning for Macon where he engineered an agreement with Alexander Shotwell and two of his business friends, Day and Butler, for eight-eighteenths interest in the same three lots at a price of four thousand dollars. The agreement carried the stipulation that Shotwell, Day and Butler, and others "would support and build in Albany as a town and place of business in preference to any other place on the Flint River." This, at last, fulfilled the conditions of the sale to Holcombe-Peck and Company of Augusta. The sales in Macon were to be paid by stock in the land company there owning thirty-five thousand acres on or near the Flint River in the Albany-Newton-Bainbridge area.

On the 20th of March, 1837, Nelson arrived, via Hawkinsville, in Albany, where letters from his brothers in Key West, his sister at Mobile, and Mother Hannah in Mystic awaited him. All were well, but Amos still wanted to go back to Mystic as his permanent home. Mother Hannah reported that Old Solomon was still living with his daughter, Mrs. Eunice Tift Crumb, but was always talking of another voyage to Key West and insited that he was needed in southwest Georgia to help Nelson fight off the red savages. Elizabeth Jane was now fifteen, Frances Amanda thirteen, and Annie King eleven years old. Of course, all had sent their undying love to Charles and Nelson.

The "Mary Emeline" had landed at the foot of Broad Street and had discharged her cargo. Nelson and Charles were very pleased with the sawmills when they took them out of their sturdy crates. The steamer took on two hundred twenty bales of cotton and was scheduled to pick up forty more bales at Bainbridge. The two hundred twenty bales were for Boyce and Company and for Holcombe-Peck and Company at one-half cent per pound, which was one-fourth cent a pound lower shipping rate than earlier shipments from the Albany area. At the same time, the shippers were saving on drayage and wharf fees as Tift had charged them none.

Nelson discounted his draft on T. C. McClay with Raymond and Allison, deducting interest at the usual rate and paying this bill in the amount of slightly over one thousand dollars. He then paid the "Mary Emeline" account of forty-six dollars, and the balance of the note in goods from the store. For additional goods and expenses for the steamer, he drew a draft on Boyce and Company of Charleston for one thousand three hundred and ninety-eight dollars due in ninety-five days from 14 March, 1837. Charles told Nelson that he was confident now that he could free his older brother from some of the administrative burden of their affairs. "Just don't try to keep it all in your head, and we will do fine. Be sure to let me have the details on every transaction that you negotiate," Charles cautioned his older brother.

The "Mary Emeline" was laid up for a few days for repairs. They had made a very good and profitable voyage downriver from Albany. A ball was being given by the Apalachicola merchants for visitors to their city, and Nelson had been invited along with Captain Watts. They put on their best "bib and tucker" and attended the colorful affair, which was well conducted and enjoyed by all. Nelson made some good business contacts. One of the men introduced to Nelson told him that he was going to St. Joseph the next day and invited Nelson to ride in the buggy with him.

"I will be very happy to make the trip with you, Sir, as I had intended to go there to see about getting some spare and missing parts for my sawmills while our boat is laid up for repairs here," Nelson replied. Colonel Robert Bereridge told Nelson that his daughter would accompany them on the trip, saying, "It will be a hard thirty-five mile ride, Mr. Tift, and we will, quite frankly, feel much more secure with a young man such as yourself riding with us. The road is not well-traveled, but there will be some travelers along the way. There are three stations where the stage stops and makes horse changes, but if we leave early enough, we may make it to our home, which is five miles this side of St. Joseph, before dark." The Colonel shook hands with Nelson and told him to meet him at the livery stable "bright and early."

The only person at the livery stable the next morning when Nelson got there was a sleepy-headed young boy who was getting a pair of fine looking black horses hitched to a nice little barouche. Nelson indentified himself to the youngster and asked if it could be Colonel Bereridge's rig that he was hitching up.

"Sho' is, Mistah. You the man what's going wid 'em to St. Joseph? Colonel said you'd be here 'bout sun-up," said the freckle-faced boy. "Wanna gimme a hand, and we'll drive 'er up to the Colonel's hotel." The two of them made short work of it and drove the rig up to the hotel over the oyster-shell street. At the door stood a beautiful young woman dressed in the height of fashion for an outing with the Colonel.

"Never heard of going on a long trip with a fashionable-dressed woman and not having a parcel of trouble," grumbled the stableboy as he drove the glistening little rig alongside the curb and got down, touched the forelock of his hair, accepted a silver coin from the Colonel, and ran back down the street.

"Ah, good morning, Nelson! May I introduce my daughter to you? My dear, I want you to meet my friend, Nelson Tift of Albany, Georgia, who was nice enough to accept my invitation to make this trip with us back home. Nelson, this is my youngest daughter, Anita. Be careful with this girl as she is a shameless flirt and has a string of broken hearts clear out to Mobile and will, no doubt, try to intimidate you as she has half the young bachelors who live in the 'Big Bend Country' of Apalachicola Bay."

Nelson took the soft, dainty little hand that was offered him and gently assisted the beautiful girl onto the spring seat, very conscious of the unbelievably breath-taking, violet-colored eyes that stole a mischievous, tantalizing look at him from beneath a perky little cap. "Will you drive until I can get myself sufficiently awake to relieve you?" asked the Colonel from the seat behind them into which he, with much difficulty and wheezing, had climbed.

"By all means, Colonel! May I say you have a splendid rig, and this pair of black horses respond as though they are excellently trained!" Nelson replied, as he sat down beside Anita, took the reins from her small, gloved hands, and "clucked" for the animals to move forward. The Colonel soon fell asleep, and the two young people talked about all the things that young people think of when they are feeling each other out and each wants to know how the other feels about such vitally important subjects as love, marriage, fashions, parties and dancing, religion, the arts, education — and maybe a little scandal. Anita skillfully guided the conversation until she knew all about Nelson, his family, his plans and his business. Nelson, on the other hand, just as skillfully found out that this little vixen had been engaged three times within the past year and was indeed leaving a trail of broken hearts everywhere she went with the Colonel. Not wanting to become yet another victim of her charms, Nelson resolved to watch his step and not over-commit himself, lest he, too, lose his heart to this designing young woman.

The horses were fed, watered, and rested at the first stage stop. While the animals were being cared for, the Colonel and the two young people also rested and washed up a bit before having a hearty meal of venison, quail, some cheese, cornbread, and homemade wine. They rested for an hour after dining, and then continued their trip. This time Nelson sat on the little "jump" seat at the rear, and the Colonel handled the team of blacks. After about an hour on the road, it became evident that one of the horses had developed a decided limp so they stopped to investigate what was wrong with him. "Nelson, will you take the other animal and ride on up to the next stage rest point and see the man who runs the place? I am well known to him, and perhaps he will come to our assistance or send us another horse." Nelson did as he was requested and rode bareback up the road towards the indicated rest stop.

"Oh, Nelson," called the girl from where she was seated in the shade of a tree by the side of the road, "please bring me back a sweet when you return." Nelson chuckled and nodded his head to acknowledge that he had heard and would comply with her request.

It was about three miles to the stage-stop. The man in charge was a little older than Nelson, short, swarthy, with high cheekbones and a noble nose. Nelson shook hands with the man, introduced himself, and gave the custodian of the stage-stop the Colonel's message. He noted that the man looked very much like an Indian who had some Spanish blood in him. When Nelson was told that the man'n name was "Anvil," Nelson noted that the name certainly fitted the man's grip, which was that of a very strong man. He was proven correct in this assumption a few minutes later when Anvil revealed that he was a blacksmith by trade.

"Mr. Tift, I 'spec the best thing we can do is to put that horse you rode over in the corral and take a fresh team back to the Colonel." Anvil indicated a pair of dappled greys. They had no trouble getting the well-behaved horses saddled, and they quickly rode back toward where the Colonel and Anita waited.

"Wait a minute, Anvil, do you have any kind of sweet in the store that I can take back to the young lady?"

"Well, I'll be doggoned! Sure. You wait here, and I'll ride back and get her some sugar crystal candy. Boy, these women," Anvil laughed and rode back toward the stage-stop. It did not take long to negotiate the switch of teams, after which the Colonel told Anvil that he would send a man back in a day or so to exchange again their teams of horses. The remainder of the trip was uneventful and was made without further mishap. They arrived at the Bereridge home just as the sun was setting in the Gulf of Mexico. Nelson spent the night at the Colonel's home and was sent into St. Joseph by buggy the next morning. Colonel Bereridge had questioned him about Albany and had evidenced great interest in being allowed to "get in on the ground floor" with the building plans for the new town. Nelson felt extremely fortunate to have gotten away from Anita without having made a declaration of sentiment, as no sooner had the word somehow gotten around that she was back home than buggies and fancy-looking thoroughbred horses with ambitious and hopeful suitors riding them started pulling into the big curved driveway in front of the colonial mansion. As the young blades hitched their mounts to the hitching racks and posts, Nelson watched with amazement and thought to himself, "There can be only one winner, and in this instance the winner might well be the loser for having won the prize of the lady's hand. She is about the most shallow, vain, selfish, childlike and demanding creature I ever saw. Beautiful, yes, but if there was ever a time when the saying the old folks have about beauty being only skin deep applies, it must be in this instance."

The general appearance of St. Joseph pleased Nelson. Of course, the cotton box materials had been as widely used here as in Apalachicola. A small cloth bag filled with attachments needed to complete the setting up of the mills in Albany was located by the clerks at the F. J. Wood and Company mill supply office. It had been inadvertantly left out of the shipment of the two mills. Mr. Wood apologized to Nelson and invited him to supper, where he was told that the company was most interested in having him act as their agent in southwest Georgia.

Nelson was introduced to Peter W. Gautier, editor of the St. Joseph *Times* newspaper and Raymond Dominde, the paper's publisher. They told him of their impending plans to have the first constitution of Florida drawn up at St. Joseph the following year. Peter Gautier explained in some detail the rivalry between St. Joseph and Apalachicola and how the threat of the "Forbes Purchases" or Spanish land grant of much of the land from Apalachicola north to three rivers, to the old Panton Leslie Trading Company, how the John Forbes Company was making "squatters" out of Apalachicola people who were afraid that the Supreme Court would decide against them and force them from their homes. Many of these people had moved or were moving to St. Joseph. Nelson also met Mr. Yarborough and Mr. Smith, who owned the shipping agency that represented Mr. John Ogden's New York and St. Joseph packets of 88 Wall Street, New York City.

Mr. Wood discussed some of the more detailed particulars of an agreement between Nelson and his company. Nelson told his new business associates that Colonel Bereridge had evidenced much interest in Albany and wanted to invest in the new trading town on the Flint River. The old Battle of New Orleans veteran was considered to be a very astute businessman by Nelson's hosts, as they had watched the Colonel's considerable business acumen demonstrated in a number of endeavors which had culminated in financial success.

Several of the younger members of the mill-firm invited Nelson down to the water with them for moonlight bathing. Nelson thought it a little cool for this sort of thing, but not wanting to be known as a "wet blanket," he went along down to the water's edge where the family of one of the young men had a strange-looking little house on wheels which they called a "bathing house" or "bath house." A horse was used to pull the peculiar little vehicle out into the water and then the family or the individual or the couple could change clothes inside the bath house and slip outside to bath in comparative privacy. For those who were really Puritan in taste, there was a trap door in the floor of the bath house that the modest one could drop through into the water and thus bathe in absolute privacy.

Nelson was wading in the surf with his trousers rolled up above his knees when the horse was led by, pulling the contraption behind. When the horse was up to his belly, he came to a stop and patiently stood still. Nelson heard feminine voices and the carefree laughter of young men and women. Now he knew why one of the young men had handed him a pair of old cut-off trousers and had winked roguishly at him and said, "You will need these, my friend." Nelson went back up on the beach where he had left the abbreviated item of clothing and quickly changed garments before he went running down toward the water where he made a great "belly buster" as he plunged into the waves and made his way out to where the excited laughter and talk was coming from in the general vicinity of the portable bath house. It was nearly impossible to identify who was who, and nobody seemed to care. It was all in good, clean fun and never had Nelson enjoyed anything more. The whole proceeding was a little risqué of course, and a short while before, Nelson knew that he would have been quite disapproving of the idea of the game he was now thoroughly enjoying.

The next morning he took the little steam engine and two-car train of the St. Joseph Canal and Lake Wimico Railroad to Greenville, Florida. He noted that this little steam locomotive was much like the one he and old Pierre had taken that day so long ago in Charleston. This one was built by Mr. M. W. Baldwin for A. Brown and Company of Philadelphia and was brand new looking. Of course, it was a "Please, don't rain" type of conveyance with no shelter from sun or rain. From Greenville, he went down the lake to Apalachicola in a boat with three young men who had been looking for a fourth "hand" to help them make the trip in their four-place open paddleboat. It was a capital adventure. Nelson had missed the fellowship of young men his own age recently and the fun in the water with them at St. Joseph the night before had whetted his appetite for more of the same. He now silently resolved to spend more time with young men and women of good moral character and to find more pleasure in this short life on earth. Nelson did not reveal to his companions in the big rowboat that he was a man who had sailed ships on the high seas and piloted steamboats on the rivers. It was enough to pull his weight with the others on their present voyage and to share in their laughter and fellowship as they literally fought their way down the lake to Apalachicola.

The "Mary Emeline" was nearly ready to depart on her upriver run by the time Nelson had rounded up the purchases he had made and got them on board. They departed from Apalachicola on a wind-and-rain swept day in March, stopping at Mt. Vernon to pick up cargo for Bainbridge. Nelson talked with his friend, Davis, who said that the name of "Mt. Vernon" was to be changed to "Chattahoochee" because the government had an arsenal at Mt. Vernon, Alabama, and one at Mt. Vernon, Florida, and wanted the latter "Mt. Vernon" changed. Nelson sent a young boy up to a store to get a present he had promised a lady. "Here is some money—just so it is in a large size for a big black woman who loves anything red." The lad came back with a beautiful pair of loud red, silk stockings that Nelson knew would make every black woman—and some white—in Albany green with envy.

The "Mary Emeline" made an uneventful trip up the Apalachicola and into the Flint. They unloaded the Bainbridge cargo at the docks there and picked up a little cargo going on toward Albany. On March 21, 1837, the "Mary Emeline" arrived at Reaton's Shoals. It was early dusk, and the crew needed to pull into shore and cut some wood for fresh fuel. The night was spent at Reaton's Shoals, and they started upstream early the next morning. They safely negotiated the lower shoal, but the upper shoal was too swift and shallow. "Get the ropes, boys, and let's suck her through," Captain Watts ordered. The men went to work and had the vessel nearly through when the boiler burst. There was nothing to do but build some supports while a few of the men went hunting and others cut wood. Nelson made it to Atkinson's and walked on into Albany from there.

It was pitch dark when Nelson saw the first flickering lamplight at the lower end of Front Street. A dog started barking and a voice sang out, "Who be ye? Speak up; I gotta bead on ye."

"Call off the dogs, Uncle Billy. It's me, Nelson Tift. The 'Mary Emeline' is stranded at Reaton's Shoals, and we have a busted boiler to boot!"

"Get back in here, yo mangy varmint," Uncle Billy yelled to the dog. He came out of the little one-room shack with the dim light. "Come on in, Nelson. I know you must be beat," the old man said kicking at his mongrel dog.

"Thank you, Billy, but I had better get on up to the store and let Charles know what has happened. How're things at the steam mill site?" Nelson asked as he climbed the muddy clay road up toward Broad Street and the store.

"Mr. Tift, was ye able to git them missing parts to the mills?" Old Billy asked as he tagged along. Nelson had always noted that the men called him M[r] being formal and asking somethi[ng]... rest of the time he was just plai[n]...

"Sure did, Billy, and now we [can] I can see the outline of the warehou[se] so you can go on back to your hous[e] for your assistance." Nelson looked [back and] saw the bobbing, weak, little light a[t] Uncle Billy's house. Nelson walked t[o the] store and called in a loud voice, "[It's] Nelson!" The front door opened after [a moment], and Nelson walked toward his brother, Charles, who stood outlined by a flickering kerosene light in the open doorway.

The next morning Charles took Uncle Billy and two "hands" with him down to the "Mary Emeline." They paddled the long rowboat with all the materials that Captain Watts had requested Nelson to send him. Charles picked up the bag of parts for the steam mills and brought them back to Albany. Nelson, Uncle Billy, and two "hands" now went to work and finished the job of putting the mills in working order.

"Build a fire in the floating mill, Uncle Billy, while I get the big mill ready," Nelson said as he and the "hands" got the last piece of equipment adjusted to the big steam mill. By the time they finished the job on the big stationary steam sawmill and went over to where Uncle Billy was working with the steam gauges on the floating mill, all was in readiness to see if the fruit of their labors was ready to be harvested. Nelson went to the controls and inspected the belting and the levers and gears. "Do we have enough steam up now, Billy?" he asked the old man.

Uncle Billy's eyes met those of Nelson, and there was a faintly perceptible nod in the affirmative. Then Nelson slowly engaged the gears and started the saw. The saw sprang into action ready to sing its song, as Nelson eased a small log into its teeth. Everything was working perfectly so far. Nelson motioned Uncle Billy to take over the controls while he went back over to the big sawmill, taking one of the "hands" with him to light up the fire and get steam up on the big boiler. He went back to join Uncle Billy, and they made a few minor adjustments until the machinery was performing exactly as they her off, Billy, and let's go back over and see ...ugh steam to find out whether the big one will ...this one," Nelson said. They went over and Uncle ...ter a quick inspection of the gauges, reported that "steam ...up." Nelson went through the same procedure as he had ...ith the floating mill, and to their great joy, everything worked out as it had on the smaller engine. They were in the sawmill business in a big way with two brand-new mills in operation.

Two days later the now familiar screech of the "Mary Emeline's" whistle split the silence of the great piney woods section that was Albany, and by the time everybody in the area was clustered on both sides of the bank at the Broad Street landing, the "Mary Emeline" came into view around the bend and nosed into her landing. A full cargo for downriver trade was waiting, and after being fully loaded, the steamer went back down to the Bay. She was scheduled to return from the Bay to Fort Gaines, as Captain Watts had some work to do on her before going on to Columbus and from there to Bainbridge and Albany. Of course, the crew could see their families and visit while the "Mary Emeline" was being repaired at Fort Gaines.

Charles was like a little boy with his first toy. He seemed pleased to operate and to be around the sawmills. Uncle Billy was just about the proudest man in Baker County, and the two Negroes held their heads high as they were recognized as men of some importance in the county. It was well known that they were being taught everything there was to know about the mills by Mr. Tift and old Uncle Billy. It soon became common knowledge that if one knew these two men, it might be possible that they would lay aside a special-cut board or maybe some cut-off material or scantlings for fireplaces on a cold evening. Nelson finally had to tell Charles that he was needed much more at the warehouse, store, landing, and with the books than he was needed at the mills, saying, "Now Uncle Billy can teach the blacks all that he wants to teach them about running the mills, loading lumber, and delivering it to the customers, but no one can teach them to run our business. I want you to concentrate more on all of our businesses and less on the sawmills. I do want you to go with me to see if we can get the floating mill from the Flint into the Muckafoonee Creek and from there into the Kinchafoonee and the Muckalee creeks.

Nearly everybody in northern Baker County had said that Nelson and old man Hawkins were out of their minds when it was said that they were trying to mount a steam engine on a floating mill. When they came to watch the two men and their two black "hands" actually mounting the lightweight engine on the rough frame they had built over two pontoon-looking boats which were twenty-five feet long and five feet wide, they were certain that the two men were out of their minds.

Old man Tison had shown Nelson how he thought they could get the contraption, as he called the floating mill, from the Flint into the desired creeks. Young Charlie Tison came down from the ferry and brought a friend with him. The friend was a "fadeaway"—strong, good-natured, and spoke good English. The arrival of Charlie Tison and his friend brought the number of men available to the desired six-man crew necessary to pole the floating mill upstream. Equipped with long, strong hickory poles, the unlikely-looking craft left Albany amid some cheers, but more catcalls, from those who believed that they would never get past the first shoals. Nelson, Charles, Charlie Tison, and his friend who had been identified as William Kennard, and the two blacks took turns with the poles, three working and three resting. It was hard work "just like keelboating!" Charles yelled. It took them two hours to pole up to the ferry at the forks where the cable had been loosened for them. Old man Tison was waiting for them and insisted on going up through the "passage" with them, saying, "You boys won't never find the place to go through if ye don't take me wid ye." It was well after sundown when they finally did get through and into the Muckafoonee. It had been back-breaking work and all the men on board were willing to concede that they would never have made it without the old man's showing them the way and goading the very devil out of them by saying repeatedly, "Now, when I was yore age, I'd'a took this contraption through by myself. You young whippersnappers just ain't got the same gumption as we had."

The moon was coming up as they, after hours of trials and tribulations under the scathing tongue of old man Tison, tied the floating mill to some cypress tree knees out about fifteen feet from the big island that stands in the middle of the lake where Kinchafoonee and Muckalee meet and form the Muckafoonee. The old man was fit to be tied when he discovered that they were not going to "fire her up" before the next morning. He said, "I don't give a Continental about it looking like rain or nothing else. Hell! I ain't hunted 'coon and 'possum all over this territory at night for nothing! Why, I know it like the palm of me hand! Come on, let's fire 'er up one time. I wanna be the first damn old man on the river to see it saw a board off a big log. C'mon now, you boys owes it to me." The old man was dead serious in making his request, and the men knew it.

"Mr. Tift," Kennard said, looking at Nelson, "I know a short cut — a good path through open and high country back to Albany — and I will be pleased to guide you back if you will let us do this for Mr. Tison. It will mean much to him to be the first of his friends to see this thing work," Nelson laughed, and both Charlie and his brother laughed with him. Without any further discussion, they went ashore and started gathering dry twigs and wood to fire up the boiler. The two blacks dragged in a sizable log they had found and set it up on the "carriage."

"We should have enough steam in a minute or so," Nelson remarked as they sat looking at the beautiful sky with its galaxies of stars. "That moon is as bright as most of our lanterns. Why, I do believe I can read a book by it," he said.

"Yes, I can even see the controls and the numbers on the instruments and gauges," Charles replied. They all sat quietly and looked at the great silent country around them. The only noises were those that were supposed to be there as a thousand frogs, dozens of alligators, legions of birds, and all manner of small furry animals sang their chorus, bellowed or screeched their challenges or mating calls, or just moved through the underbrush with slithering whispers of sound. "Steam is up!" Charles announced, and Nelson went over to the controls.

All of the sounds of animal life came to an abrupt halt as the sharp saw touched the log. All eyes on the floating mill were on the saw as it bit into the log and sang its powerful song. Only Nelson and Charles watched the framework and the pontoons for signs of stress or undue vibration. There was none, and they knew then that the mill had not been damaged during the trip upriver. Nelson drew a sigh of relief and said a quiet prayer of thanksgiving. He and old Hawkins had planned well, but he knew that, without God's help, their plans and work would have gone for naught.

The trip up through the creeks and the excitement of running the saw had been too much of a strain on the older Tison. "We will keep the fire going and let him rest until dawn, then I'll get him back down to the ferry. First let me pole you over to the Albany side of the creek where you won't have no water 'tween you and the town," young Tison told the others.

"Don't you want me to leave the blacks with you in case you have to carry your father in the morning?" Nelson asked with concern.

"Naw, thank ye. We'll be all right. You'd better be a-getting back. Why, the old man will be telling tales all up and down Pindertown by tomorrow evening letting his old friends know how he ran the first floating mill in the territory," Charlie said with a laugh. They said good night and followed Kennard into the woods, where, true to his words, there was an old single-file trail following a ridge of high ground right up to Jackson Street and into Albany where Uncle Billy was anxiously awaiting their return at the store. Nelson and Charles took the blacks and Kennard into the store where they made some coffee and had a little food.

"I am going to leave for Ft. Gaines in the morning. I plan to go out by Byron and Gillionville and on to Ft. Gaines by the Hartford Trail, so I better be getting some rest," Nelson said after they had eaten.

"How will you travel, by horseback or buggy?" Kennard asked.

"Thought I would take the buggy I traded for the other day. It seems sound enough," Nelson answered.

"If you are going by Byron and Gillionville, I can guide you part of the way, but I don't think it is a good idea to try to make the trip in a buggy at this particular season of the year," Kennard said, brushing his mane of black hair under his worn coonskin cap.

"What mode of travel would you recommend, friend Kennard?"

"First, off, you should have two mounts that are well broken to the saddle and that are not subject to running away when frightened by wild animals, snakes, or 'gators. You will need to change horses every ten miles or so lest you find you have a lame animal. I will ride one of your animals, without a saddle, until I get you headed right for Ft. Gaines, and then I will double back, using foot trails I know, to Palmyra Springs and on up the Kinchafoonee Creek to my home."

"It sure is neighborly of you to help us his way. I certainly hope we will be able to repay you for your kindness," Charles said.

"Well, in a way, you do, now and then," the dark-skinned man said mysteriously.

"How is that?" Nelson said, suddenly wide-awake.

"My friend, Moses Sherwood, and I have some men that you and your friends have been 'renting' through a friend of ours from the woods between Palmyra and Starksville. These men, as you probably already know, are not really blacks and those that are blacks are not all black," Kennard said cautiously.

"Oh, sure, we know all about the 'fadeaways' here in southwest Georgia, but we sure didn't know that these men we have been using are from the Kinchafoonee at Kennard's Landing," Charles answered.

Nelson had been quietly putting two and two together, and now he said, "Now, I see why you are so interested in the floating mill. You want us to cut your timber up at your place, don't you, Kennard?"

"Thou sayest, not I," said the dark one, throwing back his handsome head and laughing uproariously.

Nelson was up early and hastened to wash up, change his linen, and put an extra change of clothing in his bedroll. He gave last-minute instructions to Charles and went looking for Kennard who had been up for some time. He found him near the warehouse where he was working and playing with the blacks, who were making a game of floating some cargo up to the warehouse from the river. The canal water was very cold; nevertheless, Kennard and some of the "hands" were apparently having the time of their lives in the cold water. "Come on up, Kennard, and let's be on our way!" Nelson called down to him.

"Been waiting on you," the naked man yelled back, and getting out of the water, he shook himself like a wet dog and slipped into his two-piece, deerskin, trail clothes. When they got back to the store, Charles had one horse saddled and the other one equipped with a halter, bit, and a coil of rope. They rode straight on out Broad Street until they were in the deep woods at the edge of town, and then they came upon a north-westerly animal trail that was just wide enough for the horses to pass along single file. Every now and then a snake would slither across the trail, or they would see white oak runners or other type tree snakes. The birds were everywhere, rabbits were startled and hopping down the trail in front of them. The mosquitoes, horseflies, and bees were a nuisance, but it was the little black gnats that really bothered Nelson. Kennard gave a sign for Nelson to dismount and secure his horse. They eased over a little rise, on foot, and a most delightful scene met their eyes. There in a perfect little amphitheatre was a round blue hole of water where several deer were alternately munching the green grass or drinking of the water, while standing knee-deep in the blue stream that flowed from the "boil." The deer sensed the presence of man and bounded out of the beautiful little bowl-shaped glade and into the deep woods. Kennard got up from the position in which he had been watching and brushed the pine needles and red clay from his deerskin jumper.

"Blue Hole is fifty feet deep and the best drinking water this side of Blue Springs, which is on the other side of the Flint. That is Cooleewahee Creek flowing from it," Kennard said as they started back to get their mounts and bring them down to be watered. After the mounts were taken care of, the two men stripped down to the buff and Kennard "hit" the cold water. Nelson saw that his companion had one of the best bodies he had ever seen on a human being. The dark one cut through the water like a giant fish after making a perfect dive from a big cypress tree that grew over the "boil." Nelson watched as his friend went deep into the mouth of the underground river from whence the water boiled upward. He must have stayed down well over a minute before he shot to the surface, gasping and laughing at the same time. "Come on, Nelson, hit the water—but be prepared for a shock. It is really cold today!" Nelson waded out into the creek and advanced toward the boil until he was armpit deep, then he held his breath and pushed off out over the clear, deep water of Blue Hole. It was not so bad once their bodies became acclimated to the temperature of the water. They went deep into the boil and chased the big lazy fish. It was great fun, and they came out of the water fully refreshed. They dressed and got back on their horses to resume their ride.

Nelson asked William Kennard a question that had bothered him for some time. "Tell me, friend Kennard. I have heard the name 'Moses' bandied about by you and others since I first came to southwest Georgia. Just exactly who is he?"

Kennard stopped his horse in the wide place where their trail crossed a larger one running from east to west. "Byron is right up the trail about a mile. You will see several stores, a cotton gin, a grist mill, and a few houses. It was the county seat of Baker County 'til they moved the records to Gillionville for a short time while they were building the new courthouse at Newton. I will be leaving you here. There is a good trail from Byron that leads straight to the Hartford Trail. You turn west on Hartford Trail and stay on it right on into Fort Gaines on the Chattahoochee River. Now, you asked about my friend, Moses. If I did not like and trust you and Charles for the good men that you are, I would not be here with you at this moment, and because I do trust you, I will tell you about my friend," Kennard said slowly.

Chapter 5

Nelson dismounted and tied his horse alongside the one William had been riding and said, "Now, if this Moses is a runaway slave or a 'fade-away', you need not feel that you must tell me anything about him, but let me assure you that a friend of yours is a friend of mine."

"My dear friend, Moses Sherwood probably has a better education than either of us. He is the son of the celebrated Creek war chief, Menewa, and a runaway slave girl who died of a broken heart after her husband was defeated, mutilated, and left for dead after the terrible Battle of Horseshoe Bend. Moses and his twin sister were adopted by a wealthy woman of Mobile who had been his father's dearest friend. This woman once owned much land between the Flint River and Mobile — land that was taken from the Spanish, the Indians, and the trading companies to whom the Indians had given land. Panton and Leslie Trading Company was one of the big losers when Andrew Jackson forced the Creeks to sign over millions of acres of their last hunting grounds to the United States."

"But how do you explain this woman's coming into possession of all this land in Indian territory?"

"You see Nelson," Kennard answered, "my uncle, Jack Kennard, knew Rebecca Sherwood quite well. He also knew and traded with old William Panton, the great trader who represented Spain to the Indians. Now Panton and Leslie Trading Company bartered their goods to the early settlers and Indians for furs and other products of the forests. They also accepted great tracts of land when the Indians fell behind in their accounts and wanted to settle up. William Panton adopted Rebecca after she lost her parents in a boating accident on the Chattahoochee at the falls where the great Indian town of Coweta was, before Columbus was settled."

"Oh, yes, I know about William Panton; but what I do not understand is that if Moses was adopted by this rich woman, what is he doing out here now in the middle of nowhere in the backwoods of southwest Georgia?"

"Well, that is a long story, but to make it short, Rebecca took Moses and his sister, Ruth, to New Orleans where they were educated with the Creole young folk of that area. Rebecca returned to her native country, England, for a visit, and while she was gone, Chief Menewa visited his children in New Orleans. It was decided that the twins would wait until their foster mother returned to New Orleans and would tell her they thought they should return to their father's home in Okfuskee, in the northeast Alabama territory. Rebecca married an English Lord and moved from Mobile to England. The twins returned to Okfuskee and were there at the time of the Indian Removal. Ruth went west with Chief Menewa, but the old Chief still had friends in high places and wanted Moses to go to southwest Georgia where they had once met and fished on the Flint and the Kinchafoonee. Since my uncle was in Alabama and in touch with the Chief, arrangements were made for Moses to come to Kennard's Landing. When he arrived, I was the last of my family living in the area and was about at my wits' end trying to guide and lead people who had 'owned' everything in sight and now were being barely tolerated in much the same manner that they had tolerated the settlers who had eased into their lands prior to the Jackson Treaty and the Georgia Land Lotteries. Moses had the necessary leadership to sustain us when we faced emergencies and the courage and knowledge to face the impossible situation in which we found ourselves."

"But how did General Winfield Scott's army miss catching the son of a great war chief?"

"The General came personally to the landing where the trading post was located before the Jackson Treaty. Of course, we knew he was coming many hours before his arrival. Those who wanted to accept the government's bounty—and these consisted of mostly old people, the shiftless and the lame—gathered their meager belongings and waited for the army to arrive. Those who did not want to go west simply faded back into the deep woods and swamps." William Kennard paused, smiled his mischievous smile and added, "But you want to know why

Moses chose to stay and talk with the General instead of fading away with the others?"

"I know that there is a catch somewhere, but I'll ask anyway. Why did Moses stay?" Nelson asked in a resigned tone.

"Because Andy Jackson knew very well where Moses was. He had shaken hands and talked with him, had spent the night in the same tent with him just a few miles from Kennard's Landing at old Herod's Town when the General and Menewa were on their way to fight the Seminoles in 1818. General Scott brought official papers from Andrew Jackson that would forever prevent anyone from making life uncomfortable or even unpleasant for the son of Chief Menewa."

"Wonder why Jackson did not help Chief Menewa? I heard that the Chief was heartbroken over having to leave his home," Nelson mused half to himself.

"He did try to prove how Menewa had helped the Army in the Seminole wars and in many other ways after his horrible wounds from Horsehoe Bend had healed and after the bitterness of defeat had passed away. But the stigma of the awful massacre of Fort Mimms had been falsely attributed to Menewa instead of to the half-breed Creek, Wiliam Wetherford, who had actually planned and led the Red Sticks in the largest massacre of settlers and soldiers ever perpetrated by the American Indians. The public and the leaders of the United States demanded that Menewa be taken with his followers." Kennard paused and said reflectively, "Nelson, I remember an article that was in the Mobile newspaper, telling about Menewa's last night before he was taken west. It said, 'All the Creeks were forced to leave Okfuskee, including Menewa, who had received a personal promise from high authority to the contrary.' On the night before he left for exile, he spent the night with his children, and the next morning said to his friend, Jack Kennard, 'Last evening I saw the sun set for the last time, and its light shine upon the tree-tops, and the land and the water that I am never to look upon again.' Then he walked away, led by his beautiful, faithful little daughter, Ruth. He was an old man, horribly scarred, wounded many times." The soft voice of William Kennard broke with suppressed emotion as he finished the story.

Nelson cleared his throat and said, "You mean that Moses can, without fear of being picked up by the authorities, come to Albany, come into my store, and visit with me?"

"Albany, New York, Albany, Georgia, it would make little difference and he has the papers to prove it," Kennard laughed and handed to Nelson the rope holding the animal he had been riding.

"Nelson, did you ever hear about the Spanish land grant to the Panton and Leslie Trading Company? Good, well, old William Panton and most of his partners have passed on, and his company is now the John Forbes Company. Moses' foster mother was a part of the old company and has retained considerable interest in the John Forbes Company. Now you know that thousands of acres of land will go to Moses and his foster mother if the Supreme Court decides against the settlers and land owners from three rivers to Apalachicola Bay," Kennard said.

"Then what you are saying—that there is a very good chance that Moses will someday be wealthy and will live with me in Albany? I just wonder why he has not been to see me before?" Nelson asked.

"Have you sent him an invitation, Nelson?" asked the amused Kennard. Nelson secured the rope to the ring on his saddle and looked up to answer but William Kennard had silently departed. The thick bushes quivered for a moment where he had entered them. Then there was no sound, save the twittering of small birds and the scurrying of a furry creature.

Byron was much as it had been described. The stranger stopped and introduced himself to the proprietors of the stores and quoted them some prices on merchandise he had coming up from Apalachicola. "But Mr. Tift," asked one of the men, "how in the world can you quote us such low prices? Certainly, we will be happy to buy at that price, and we will be coming over to Albany to see you quite soon." Several farmers came into the stores while Nelson was there and he was introduced to them. One man was going in a buggy to Gillionville and said he would be happy to have company on the ride with him.

Jerimiah Walters asked Nelson to tie the horses to the back of his buggy and ride up on the seat with him. After this was done, they started off down the little wheel-bearing road toward Gillionville. "Mr. Tift, I have been all the way to Fort Gaines on horseback, and I can tell you that it gets mighty scary down in those swamps at night. I did not see many people between here and there, but the ones I did see were very friendly and hospitable, and I found the citizens at Fort Gaines to be well-bred and most cultured."

"How long ago did you make the trip to Fort Gaines, Mr. Walters?"

"About six weeks ago. I wish I could get away to go with you on the trip over there."

"Have you been over to Albany, Mr. Walters?"

"Yes, sir, Mr. Tift. I was over there several weeks ago. You were downriver, and I talked with an old fellow there at the store. You know we all believe and pray that you will have a nice town there on the river."

"Well, thank you for saying so, Brother Walters. We are going to strive mightily to do just that. I hope I am at home the next time you call on me." It was getting a little late in the afternoon when they arrived at Gillionville. There were about twenty good-sized houses, some of them smaller cabins in a row behind the larger ones. They went on by this cluster of buildings for about a mile until they came to several small buildings at the intersection of a north-south-trail which crossed the larger Hartford Trail. This was Gillionville, and from his first impression, Nelson thought it compared favorably in size to Albany, except for the steamboat business, warehouses, and mills. Mr. Walters introduced him to John Gillion and Nelson asked that gentlemen about the missing papers he had been told about at the County Seat.

"Mr. Tift! I have been hoping to see you. Where are you headed? It will be dark shortly, and I would like for you to have supper with us and spend the night," Gillion invited.

"Thank you, Mr. Gillion. I am on my way to Fort Gaines and would be most pleased to accept your generous offer for supper and to spend the night, but only on the condition that you will let me return the favor when you visit Albany," Nelson replied, thinking how fortunate he was to find John home instead of down at Newton. All of the storekeepers he met evidenced great interest in purchasing supplies from him rather than using the long supply line over the Hartford Trail from Hawkinsville.

"We are most interested in the river traffic and will help in any way we can. We have heard of your attempts to get the mail and a stagecoach on this side of the river, and we will help you in that endeavor also," one of the merchants volunteered.

That night after a good meal of vegetables, corn bread, and quail, they sat by lamplight and looked through a sheaf of old documents—none of which, it turned out, were of interest to Nelson or the town of Albany.

"How far did we come on the trail from Byron to here, John?" Nelson asked.

"Oh, about ten miles, give or take a few. You crossed two little creeks, Kiokee, and Tallassee, on your way here, and tomorrow you have to go through one of the worst places you will have to pass between here and Fort Gaines. That is the Chickasawhatchee swamp. Why, we have had wagons loaded with supplies for Concorde, Whitney, Bluffton, Blakely, and Fort Gaines held over here for a week sometimes waiting for high water to go down so's they could get through. They usually send out advance scouts before they sent the wagon trains, and they just don't try it in bad weather. That Itchaway-Notchaway stream and the Pachitla above where it flows into the Notchaway are real bad medicine and can be like a boar hog in mating season when the high water is up. There is, however, a floating ferry down where the first county seat of Early County was some years ago, right about where Neal's Creek comes into the Pachitla at Whitney, which was called Pachitla when it was county seat."

"John, you said that we crossed the Tallassee Creek. Do you know what that Indian term means in English?"

John looked nervously at his wife who was getting two little boys ready for bed. She looked up, and Nelson noted for the first time her dark eyes, straight, jet-black, hair, and the beautiful high cheek bones of her deeply tanned face. She smiled patiently and said in a soft voice, "Mr. Tift, I have told this man of mine a score of times that Tallahassee and Tallassee both have to do with an old town that has been abandoned."

The morning came quickly, and after he dressed, Nelson was given hot coffee, hoe cakes, eggs, and fatback fried in corn meal for breakfast. One of the little Gillion boys was having to help his mother as punishment for being impudent. He had told Nelson, "It don't make me no nevermind. Iffen I does, my Ma won't lemme," after Nelson had told him that he would let him ride on his steamboat if he wanted to when his folks brought him over to Albany.

"Mr. Tift, I just don't know what we are going to do with this one," the Mother said apologetically. He plays with some rough little boys who go to the one-room schoolhouse with him, and he picks up the terrible language you just heard. We punish him, but he goes right back and comes home with more of the same."

"Well, Mrs. Gillion, if you will let me take him aboard the 'Mary Emeline', he will find out that most men are trying to improve their use of the language because they did not have a concerned mother and a teacher in a one-room schoolhouse to teach it to them," Nelson replied and got up from the table thanking his host and hostess for their hospitality.

Nelson went outside. It was a beautiful day — a little cool, but that would keep the insects away. John was up on his horse and had Nelson's horses outside all ready to go. John led the way to the dark and mysterious Chickasawhatchee swamp. The Hartford Trail went right up to the edge of the first little creek, and then it wandered around like a ship without a rudder in a high wind. "Wagons can make it today with oxen pulling them," John joked as they made their way over the floating bridge that crossed Chickasawhatchee Creek's main channel. This "bridge" was merely a contraption formed by lashing good-sized logs together for the animal or wagon to cross. Attached to sturdy magnolia trees on each side of the channel, it could float with the rising water or lie flat in the mud when the creek was down.

"How long will a 'bridge' of this type last?" Nelson asked.

" 'Cording to the rainfall. It might wash out at the first big gully-washer and again might last two or three years, with a little help now and again. Let's be careful and lead the horses across. Water moccasins love to live and breed in these floating bridges, and every now and again a bull 'gator will crawl up on the top side and want to take over. I ain't about to argue with no fifteen-footer, are you, Nelson?"

"Not me, John," Nelson answered as he led his horses off the floating bridge, talking soothingly to them to keep them from getting excited. The two men shook hands, and Nelson rode westward down the Hartford Trail while John went back to Gillionville and his family. The trail to Fort Gaines was a sandy, wheel-bearing road which pushed the jungle-like forest back eight to ten feet on each side, but the tops of the trees seldom let light through to the road. The branches met over it, forming a tunnel-like opening through them. Nelson thought to himself that the sun probably had not shone on this road since the big herds of heavy animals had made it into a trail, back before the time of the American Indians. The horse he was riding reared up a little and shied away from the right hand side of the road where there was water on that side nearly at the level of the road. He saw a great bullfrog that had been partially swallowed by a snake with only his head and his front feet sticking out of the snake's mouth. The frog was croaking loudly while trying to swim out of the death grip of the snake, using the pitifully inadequate power of those feet. The big snake calmly swallowed the frog bit by bit at irregular intervals, merely by a slight shifting of his hold on the frog. To Nelson it seemed that the big snake had the head of a large bull frog and two small feet under his lower jaw. It took some time to calm the animals, after which they moved on down the road.

The sun was now somewhere above the trees which had Spanish moss hung from every limb. It was spring, and everything was in bloom. The sweet aroma of the bay tree blossoms were just a smaller version of the big magnolia blossoms, which were as big as a child's head. The bay blossoms were more the size of a small clinched fist, and the color of ivory rather than beautiful white of the magnolia. The honeysuckles, water lillies, dogwoods, jasmine, Cherokee roses that lined the trail, and scores of beautiful flowers and ferns that Nelson had never seen before left him with the feeling that this, truly, could have been the Garden of Eden. Off the sides of the trail were little cleared fields that were under cultivation, and every now and then a farmer could be seen, following a mule and plow, walking in the newly created furrow of dark, rich earth that the plow was turning. Each farmer that saw Nelson signaled him to wait for a moment and came over to the trail to have a talk with him. In each instance, it was apparent that the farmer was just wanting to talk with someone from the "outside." Nelson noted that there seemed to be few blacks and asked a Mr. Brown, who was wrinkled and sun-burned from years of having been exposed to the merciless rays of the sub-tropical sun, where all the slaves were.

"Well, Sir, me and my old lady and the biggest of our chil'ren are the only 'slaves' I knows of hereabouts. There's several families that own a bonded man or a slave or two, but they ain't about to waste them behind a plow. Where we come from over around Savannah, all the big plantation owners has lots of slaves to do the house and field work. 'Course, as you know, them big planters is already abuying up small farms and stringin' them together into plantations over this way. They will send plenty of slaves over here later to do the plantation work."

"But Mr. Brown, you have gone to all the back-breaking work of clearing and taming this fertile land. Why do you fellows sell out to the big planters?"

"Mr. Tift, you are new in this territory. You most likely don't know that many a man is clearing and planting on land that he just don't have a real good and sound title to. Sometimes it's land that he did not draw in the lottery but kinda acquired-like. When that planter shows up with the properly registered title to the land, well, the best the man who is caught squatting on the land can hope for is to be allowed to stay on as a sharecropper or as the overseer for the planter."

"Well, I'll tell you right now, my friend, if this ever happens to you, I would feel most fortunate to have a man of your ability and caliber join me in my venture to Albany. You won't have to bring anything with you except your family and whatever personal belongings you want to bring in your wagon. We need good, hard-working families, and you can work out any kind of business arrangement you care to with Tift and Company. I must be getting on down towards the Itchaway-Notchaway; it has been a real pleasure talking with you, and I will look forward to having you come to see me in Albany," Nelson said and waved goodby to Mr. Brown, who had gone back toward his waiting horse and plow.

Itchaway-Notchaway Creek, which the old gentlemen running the grist mill had said meant "the place where the deer sleeps," was even larger than the Chickasawhatchee, but it had a log bridge built over it at a narrow spot just above the dam. One black boy and his half-breed companion were fishing under the mill. Nelson saw one of them rear back on his pole as a four-foot alligator gar tore his line all to pieces. The big gar swam away on top of the rushing water as if nothing had happened. This enraged the little boy, who tore along the top of the dam yelling curses and defiance at the big fish.

The traveler ate a hearty meal at the Notchaway Tavern and was tempted to stay the night there but decided to move on a little farther, as he wanted to make Fort Gaines the next day before darkness set in. The mother of the little half-breed "fisherman" was a fine-looking Indian woman of immense proportions and, Nelson thought, a very fine backwoods cook. She told him that the Indians called Fort Gaines "A Con-Hollo-Way Tal-lo fa" and said it meant "Highland Town."

It was about five miles from the tavern to the voting precinct in the Morgan-Concorde area, which proved to be more or less a wide place in the road where another road crossed. Nelson stopped in the wide clearing and talked with two merchants who operated "general stores" which stood at the edge of the clearing. The two merchants introduced him to several men nearby, and they discussed the possibility of buying merchandise from Nelson. One of them was Jonothan Neal from the town of Whitney, which he said was about four miles down the Hartford Trail on Pachitla Creek. Mr. Neal invited Nelson to ride with him in his wagon so that they could talk together and let Nelson's horses rest a little at the same time. Nelson noted that the man had bought some farm equipment which lay neatly stacked in the bed of the wagon. Nelson thanked Mr. Neal for his kind invitation and after tying his mounts to the back of the wagon, climbed up on the spring seat with its owner.

"Mr. Tift, I hope you will do my family the honor of spending the night with us at our humble abode. We are a very modest community although we were the center of activity some few years ago when the county seat and the courthouse of all of Early County were built there."

"My goodness, you mean to tell me that the Early County Courthouse was up here before there was a Baker or Decatur County?"

"Yes, Siree!" said the old boy with some touch of pride in his voice. Warming to the task, he continued to give Nelson a little of the local history and gossip. "You see, Mr. Tift, at the 1823 session of the Georgia Legislature, a new county was formed out of the southern part of Early County, down on the Spanish Florida boundary line. It was named Decatur County. This change brought on a need to change the courthouse site of Early County. Sam Jackson, Joseph Grimsley, and Wright Sheffield were appointed commissioners to select a new location and erect temporary buildings. They selected a very pretty place in the little town of Blakely and built a temporary courthouse. The second courthouse was built by James G. Collier and James D. Gresham for about two thousand dollars in 1835. Of course, the last court was held at our little courthouse in June of 1824 by Judge Harris. T. G. Holt was the solicitor general, Smith was still the Sheriff, McBryde was clerk, and, if I remember right, Martin Wood was foreman of the Grand Jury."

"What kind of bridge do you have across the Pachitla, Mr. Neal?"

"Well, we still have the same ferry that I helped my father and grandfather build a few years back. It's called Neal's Ferry because Neal's Creek joins the Pachitla just above the ferry. You know, Mr. Tift, we have had a terrible time trying to keep the roads and bridges open between Tinsley's Ferry on the Flint and the banks of the Chattahoochee River."

"Mr. Neal, it must have helped a little when Baker County was formed off of this end of Early County in 1826. I mean, didn't the people in the new county help with the work on the roads over their way toward the Flint?"

"Yes, sir, Mr. Tift, it sure did. We had to do a little reshuffling over this way. They appointed Zachariah Cowart commissioner of roads in place of Bryant Sheffield. H. Studstill and John Phillips were appointed to help Cowart mark out a new road from the Chattahoochee to the Flint. At the next term of court, the commissioners reported that they had marked out the road to the Baker County line on lot of land number 396 in the sixth district, passing through lot number 190 in the seventh district at Pachitla, which is now called Whitney. These comissioners were appointed by the new grand jury to secure the necessary materials and hands to get the road built and to appoint the necessary overseers to superintend the workers. Of course, they followed the existing roads and trails as much as they could and just improved those portions of the new road. They did have to make a big detour at Dr. McIntosh's store, following a more southerly course, crossing Spring Creek at Arthur Sheffield's ford and coming on up to cross Timmon's ferry on Notchaway Creek, and—"

"Hold on my friend," Nelson pleaded. "I do believe you are talking about the road from Blakely. My goodness, I thought you understood that I am headed towards Fort Gaines?"

"Ah, Mr. Tift, please forgive me, I do not have many opportunities to converse with educated men like yourself from the 'outside', and I must have become rattled and overcome by the sound of my own voice. Well, no harm done. There is a very good little trail that was built especially for the courthouse from the Hartford Trail. It goes on to Fort Gaines, and all you have done by coming this way is miss that miserable Lewis Bridge, which is up-creek through the swamp and on the main road above here. Now in the morning I will ride with you over to Nubbintown and get you back on the Hartford Trail to Fort Gaines."

"You mean they actually cut a road from the Hartford Trail through the swamps to the new courthouse here at your little town! When did they do this, Mr. Neal?"

"Yes, Sir. During the July term of court in 1824, a petition was presented to the court asking for the appointment of commissioners to view the ground and mark a road from Erwin's Ferry on the Chattahoochee near Fort Gaines to our home and the new courthouse on the Pachitla at Neal's Creek. The Court appointed Samuel Gainer, General William Dill, and my father, Jonothan Neal, commissioners with authority to examine the country through which the proposed road would be built and to mark out the same. If, in their judgment, the road would be of public convenience, they were to report to the next term of court," the old man pulled his horse up abruptly as a large buck deer bounded across the road in front of the wagon, clearing the road in one graceful leap, his white tail disappearing into the swamp on the other side of the road. "Giddeup, Hoss!" the old man clucked, urging his animal forward again toward some buildings in a wide place some distance down the road. Nelson noted the little well-kept graveyard on the left side of the road as they entered the little village on the Pachitla Creek. The big, unpainted church sat on the right side a little farther down the road.

"Mr. Neal, you were telling me about a new road that was proposed. Did they ever build it?"

"Oh, yes. A road was built from Hartford Trail starting about three miles west of the Pachitla at Lewis Bridge and running down-creek until it reached the spot below where Neal's Creek meets the Patchitla. This is where the courthouse had been built and where Freeman D. Carden still has his store. The other merchants went to the new county seat at Blakely or elsewhere after it was decided to change the location." Mr. Neal pulled his rig up to the edge of the little floating ferry that was built to rise or fall with the waters of the Pachitla.

Nelson spent most of the evening meeting new people at the church, and they talked by lamplight until nearly midnight. He met J. B. Stephens who was a few years older than Nelson and from Bridgeport, Connecticut. Stephens told Nelson that he, too, had come to this country through Augusta but that he had come down from Philadelphia on the great wagon road, all the way to Augusta, with other pioneers from the northern reaches of the Atlantic Coast. They had all used Augusta and Hawkinsville (Hartford) as their "jumping off place" into the new Indian Lands and had gotten so scattered from each other that in all probability they would never see each other again. This was due to the fact that they had all acquired land that was widely separated and scattered all over southwest Georgia. Nelson also met a Mr. Thigpen, Mr. Whiddon, Mr. and Mrs. Cobb, Mr. Bass, Mr. R. J. McClary and members of his family, and a sturdy young man named Elisha Hatcher who said that he had come up from Apalachicola on the steamboat, "The Old Tallahassee" several years back and had "won" two hundred fifty acres of land near his present neighbors, in a card game at the riverboat town of Sneads. Hatcher claimed that it had taken him over a month to locate the land and find out if he really had title to it. The men questioned Nelson as to what he might know about what the Central Bank of Georgia was doing making out suits against the citizens of southwest Georgia on notes that had two or three endorsers. These notes involved the ownership of vast tracts of land and farmers were getting uneasy about the "foreign" surveyors, who frequently came through looking into land claims for the bank.

"Mr. Tift, we are getting as suspicious as the Indians used to be about these men with their equipment that the Indians called 'land stealers' because every time one of them showed up with a compass and transit and went over the Indian's land, the Indian lost his land," young Hatcher said.

"I intend to talk with the people at Fort Gaines about this very matter. I understand that some of the larger merchants and landowners at Fort Gaines and some of them at Blakely are being hard hit by the Central Bank. Now, from what I can gather, the bank has let out too many 'bad risk' loans on land that never was properly surveyed or registered. The town fathers of the larger town want more good people to gravitate to their villages and towns, and we do not have banks in these places. The only way the farmer and small landowner has of getting financed is through the big Central Bank of Georgia. Naturally, the bank has asked the most prominent man of the village or town to vouch for the person seeking the loan, which is probaby just twenty-five to fifty dollars on from two hundred fifty acres to five hundred acres of choice land. If the farmer has a bad first year and leaves the country, then the bank wants to go back on the most prominent of the three co-signers, being the same man in nearly every instance. Now this prominent man is already land-poor and trying to sell land himself, not repossess or foreclose for more land. The big lawsuits will reveal that more than half of the land has not been properly certified. Families are living on, clearing, and building on the wrong land all over south Georgia. The prominent men will be relieved of some of this responsibility of being sole co-signers at the bank or the well-known men will refuse to go on anyone's note and will then petition the state to let them form their own small local banks. Now, you see, if the suits being brought by the citizens against the Central Bank of Georgia are allowed to get into court, the bank will very likely come out the big loser."

"You know, Mr. Tift, we have argued this thing back and forth and have been unable to form any sort of an opinion as to whether the bank or the leading merchants are at fault in this thing. Joel W. Perry of Blakely is one of the most astute men in these parts, and I was privileged to hear him talk on this very same subject over at Grimsley's Mill several weeks ago. Mr. Perry, like you, is an educated man and has a real flair for the legal aspects of this case. He reasons the whole thing out very much as you just did," Jonothan Neal said slowly.

"About how old is this church?" Nelson asked, looking around at the frame building with the plain altar and the steps that led up to the balcony.

"It was built at the same time as the courthouse. I'd say about twelve or thirteen years ago, wasn't it, Brother Neal?" replied one of the men. The group decided to break up the discussion for the night as midnight was fast approaching.

Mrs. Neal had hot coffee waiting for them when they arrived at the Neal home, and while Nelson and her husband sipped their beverage, the thoughtful woman filled a wash tub with warm, soapy water and left it before the fire in the fireplace of the spare room where Nelson would spend the night. Never had a nice warm bath been more appreciated. Nelson took full advantage of this thoughtfulness. He slept like a baby and was up when he heard the Neals stirring about just after daylight. After a good breakfast, Jonothan rode with Nelson over the road toward the place he called "Nubbintown," which was four miles west on an intersection of the Cuthbert-to-Newton trail and the Harford Trail.

"Mr. Tift, we enjoyed having you with us last evening and this morning. Please stop by to see us again when you come back this way. That little store down there at the crossroads is all there is to Nubbintown. Most of the land around here belongs to folks in Cuthbert and Blakely. I must be getting on back home, so I will say good-bye to you, Sir." Nelson shook hands with the helpful Neal and rode on towards the forlorn-looking little log structure which sat like a sentinel at the roadside. Three blacks, two of whom were a little more copper than black, were watching a spectacle of nature such as Nelson had never before witnessed, and that few people ever see. Present also was one white man about Nelson's age, a woman who peered out at him from beside the single door to the store, and two little white girls who put their fingers on their lips and looked up as the stranger rode into their "yard."

The largest girl silently slipped over to Nelson and said, "Shhhhh! I am Elizabeth Smith, and I'm three years older than my four-year-old sister, Mary." Nelson quietly turned his horses and tied them to a tree at the edge of the clearing. He went forward to stand and look over the white man's shoulder at a most unbelievable sight — a big black snake with yellow rings at intervals on his five-foot length had a three-foot-long timber rattlesnake in a death grip just behind its head. The white man squatting down in front of Nelson slowly got up and turned to the new arrival.

"Good day, Sir. I am Ben Smith," he whispered, "lately of Greene County. That is my wife in the doorway of the store, and these two girls are our children. That is my black boy over there, and those two with him live back in the woods. Can we be of service to you?" Smith was still whispering, not wanting to startle the snakes, although these appeared oblivious to the presence of humans.

"I am Nelson Tift from Albany. What is happening here, Mr. Smith?"

"Oh, yes, Albany. We heard about you'all over there on the Flint. I believe you are from up north in Connecticut, somebody allowed. Well, welcome to Nubbintown, such as it is. That is a big king snake. He can and does kill and swallow any snake in these parts, including big rattlers like the one he is fixing to swallow right now. Watch him closely. I have heard of this all my life, but this is the first time I have actually witnessed it," Mr. Smith whispered excitedly as he resumed his squatting position in the little circle of mesmerized watchers. They sat in the sun at a crossroad in an obscure, out of the way, God-forsaken spot in Early County, and watched one of nature's most dramatic phenomena played out to its bitter end. There was no sound save the bated breath of the intent spectators; the dust of the struggle covered everything, including the two snakes. At the least predictable moment, often after five minutes of absolute inactivity, the jaws of the king relaxed just enough to turn the head of the rattler a little more towards the direction in which the king had to have it in order to swallow. The big rattler fought with every ounce of power in his elongated frame, but the skill, patience, and strength of the king would not be denied. Slowly and nearly imperceptibly the king turned the rattler around and began the swallowing process until only the six rattles and a "button" remained visible. The rattlesnake fought to the bitter end and rattled loudly until he had disappeared into the maw of the king snake.

No one said a word. They all took another deep breath, their eyes round with wonderment. "Will you kill the king now?" Nelson asked Mr. Smith in a hushed voice.

"Oh, no, Mr. Tift, he is worth his weight in gold to us around this store. Other snakes will not knowingly come around as long as he is in charge of the territory that he has won for himself. We only hope that he will stay with us," Smith answered quickly and escorted Nelson inside the store, which, when his eyes became accustomed to the darkness, Nelson perceived was nearly depleted of stores and supplies.

"I will have to apologize for the bareness of the larder and the shelves, Mr. Tift. We have fallen on hard times here, and I am afraid I was naive enough to believe a man who wanted to rid himself of this location desperately enough to tell me lies about the possibilities here," Mr. Smith said with a sorrowful shake of his head. The little woman at his side nodded her head in agreement and shifted her snuff about under her lip.

"Why, Mr. Smith, are you inferring that you were cheated and sent off into the swamps of southwest Georgia on false pretenses?"

"We was adoing well up in Greene County, Mr. Tift, when this man, well-known by my old man there, talked him into trading our blacksmith shop and all the tools for this worthless grant of two hundred fifty acres and this store on the crossroads from nowhere to never-never and out here in the middle of nothing," little Mrs. Smith said, shifting her snuff again, this time in a most interesting change from upper to lower lip, accomplished by a most dexterous involvement of her tongue and a sudden movement of the lips that defied detection.

"Yea, and what's worse is that we have no means to purchase or transport goods here. I feel that if we had a decent stock of goods, we would get some trade, for there are many families back on the creeks hereabouts," added Mr. Smith. Nelson thought for a moment and wrestled with his better judgment. It was no use, for he had been down this road before, only it had been Nelson Tift in the position the Smiths found themselves in now. He remembered how lost and hopeless he had felt when Pierre, and later Oscar Danforth, had come to his rescue with supplies to keep him in business.

Nelson cleared his throat and said, "Mr. Smith, let me see your grant of the two hundred fifty acres. I may be in a position to get you a new supply of merchandise for this store and get it over to you from my place in Albany by wagon."

"Oh, Lordy be! I hopes so," said the little woman as she hurried into a shed at the back end of the store and brought back an official-looking packet of documents which she handed to Nelson. There was a map, very official looking, which carried the magnetic variation of five degrees east. The "Received eighteen dollars" recording fee was signed by a Mr. Clayton. It was for lot number ninety-three, which was two hundred fifty acres of Pachitla Creek. The map also showed four small branches and creeks flowing into the Pachitla. The map was drawn on a scale of twenty chains to an inch and read, "State of Georgia: the above plat is a representation of that tract or lot of land, situated in the fourth district in the county of Early, containing two hundred and fifty acres, which is known and distinguished in the plan of said district by the number 93.

                      Surveyed on 11 day February 1820
                      By William F. Wilkins, Surveyor

Jno McSwain
        CC
Asa McNeil

                    Daniel Sturgis"

Nelson read the piece of paper carefully and said, "This grant seems to be in order, but there should be another deed-like document that goes with it." The woman went back out of the store and soon returned with another document to hand to Nelson. It was also in order and properly executed, saying that lot 93 in the 4th district of Early had been granted to Mr. Ben Smith and was signed by Secretary of State.

"Mr. and Mrs. Smith, on the strength of these documents, I am willing to send you a two-horse wagon full of merchandise. I can see that you need it badly, if you are to survive in business. I will choose the merchandise for you and have it loaded on our steamer to Fort Gaines and sent from there by wagon, within forty days, if the water in the rivers is at navigable level during that time. Of course, if the rivers are not navigable, I will send all the way from my warehouse in Albany to you by two-horse wagon."

The man and woman looked at each other. They were not farmers; they never had been. He was just a blacksmith turned store-keeper. "Mr. Tift, I take it that you are offering to trade me a wagonload of merchandise for our two hundred fifty acres and this store. This is more than fair, but we would like to know if you would consider putting an anvil, bellows, and the usual blacksmith shop tools and equipment in that wagon instead of about half of those goods just so that we can have my trade to fall back on in case we turn out to be poor merchants?"

Nelson smiled his understanding smile and took out his notebook to write a reminder to himself of the transaction. He made sure to list the blacksmith equipment and tools that these good people wanted. He figured this was a profitable transaction for both parties. As they were saying good-bye to each other, Nelson told Mr. Smith, "I will see that you get your supplies and the blacksmith shop tools. If, after a reasonable time, you feel that you do not want to stay here, get your belongings and blacksmith shop and tools together in your wagon and come to Albany. I will stake you to a new start in your own shop on Front Street, right on the Flint River near the steamboat landing."

"But Sir, what could I give you in exchange for such a move?"

"Brother Smith, if I am to have land down here, I will also need to run a store, and I think that this place, in time, will be a good business spot. Therefore, if you decide to come to Albany and open up a blacksmith shop, lock this place securely before you leave and get a friend to watch it for you while you bring me the deed and the keys. I will try to see you on my way back if I come this way. Good day to you all," Nelson said as he rode westward.

The road was still wheel-bearing and in good condition. Nelson had noted that this was usually the case when farming activity was evident along the route being traveled. Cotton cultivation was now evident on both sides of the road, and he met some traffic. About an hour after leaving the Smith store, he saw the top of a large barn, several outbuildings, and a double-pen log cabin built of squared logs. As he drew closer, he could hear all the farm noises of chickens, cows, and horses. A farm bell tolled out its message to the fields and swamps that a stranger was on the place. A big windmill stood back of the log house, and it creaked as the wind turned the vanes. Nelson looked up at the hand-built structure and marvelled at man's ingenuity, remembering the scientific-sounding phrase his teacher had used when referring to windmills, "A chimerical project or notion" he had called them.

Dogs began to bark, and a boy and a woman, who looked as if she might be his mother, came out of the dog-run of the house and stood watching the strangers approach.

"Good day, stranger. Won't you come inside and set awhile? We are the Cowart family, and you'd be more'n welcome to stop with us," the neat looking woman said, showing an even row of white teeth as she spoke.

Nelson climbed down from his mount and carefully tied both animals to a hitching post by a watering trough filled with cool, clean water. "Thank you, Ma'am. I am Nelson Tift from Albany. I am obliged to you for your offer, but I would just like to speak with Mr. Cowart if that is possible," he said as he removed his hat and watered his animals.

"Amaziah will be along presently. I suppose you heard our farm bell as you came across Cowart's branch. We always ring the bell for fires and emergencies as well as when we have visitors." Mrs. Cowart patted her hair and took off her apron and said, "Just once in my lifetime I would love to have someone warn me that company is coming so that I would have time to fix up a little. It seems that I am always a wreck when a body does come to see us." The pretty little woman laughed as she led her visitor up on the wide porch just as a big man rode into the yard on a mule that he had been plowing. Mrs. Cowart murmured her excuses to Nelson, put her little poke bonnet back on her head, and went out to speak with her husband.

Amaziah was six feet tall, heavy of legs and shoulders, and a little stooped from constant work in the forest and field. His big hands were calloused from the plowlines, the axe handle, and the hundreds of menial tasks that confront the sod-busting farmer from "can to can't" every day of the year. After introductions, Cowart asked the visitor what brought him to their area.

"I am on my way to Fort Gaines to see Captain Watts about our steamboat and to talk to the merchants there about selling wholesale merchandise to them," Nelson answered.

"Oh, yes, Mr. Nelson Tift; now I have you placed. Mother, this is the young man who is settling that new town over on the Flint near Tinsley's ferry. Oh, Mr. Tift, I do hope you saw the folks trying to run that store down at the crossroads. They seem to need someone like yourself to advise and help them."

"Mr. Cowart, I did meet and talk to Mr. and Mrs. Smith and arrangements have been made to completely re-supply them. I will appreciate it, if you good people will circulate the news around that within three or four weeks you are going to have a first-class store in your community." Nelson thought a moment before he asked, "How many acres do you have under cultivation, Mr. Cowart?"

"Well, let's see. I have a brother south of here who has a thousand acres, of which about three hundred acres are cleared and in row crops. Me and the boys have nearly twenty-five hundred acres up in this end of the county, but we have only five hundred acres or so cleared and in cultivation." Amaziah paused and then asked a question that rather startled Nelson, "What is the name of your steamboat? Is it a stern-wheeler? How many bales of cotton can it take downriver?"

"Amaziah, you should be ashamed asking Mr. Tift all those personal questions when you hardly know him well enough to say hello. For shame on your manners, Sir!" little Mrs. Cowart said in an embarrassed voice, for she was aware that women of good breeding did not castigate their husbands in the presence of polite company.

Nelson laughed and said soothingly, "Oh, not at all, Mrs. Cowart." Although surprised at the question, Nelson replied enthusiastically, "Ships and steamboats are a big part of my life, and I will talk about them any time anyone will listen to me." It happened that Amaziah was also a devoted disciple of ship and boat lore, so the two had a mutual interest that kept them talking for two hours until Nelson remembered that he needed to be on his way westward along the trail to Fort Gaines. Amaziah insisted on riding out to the next crossroad with Nelson, and they resumed their talk about the land, crops, politics, and most of all, Amaziah's great love for steamboats.

"My friend Bass, lives over 'tween Pachitla and the store — someday he and I plan to buy us some sort of steamboat," Amaziah said.

"Why don't you both just wait until I buy my next one, and you can go in with me and be my partners?" Nelson said in a good-natured manner.

"You are joshing with me!"

"Not really. If you really want to be a partner when the time comes, I will be happy to have you with me in a joint venture," Nelson said slowly and deliberately, looking at Mr. Cowart directly and seriously.

"By golly, you really mean it, don't you, Nelson?"

"Absolutely! You just save your money, my friend, as this might come to pass sooner than you think." They had arrived at the spot where a smaller trail crossed the Hartford Trail. "This it?" Nelson inquired.

"Yep, this is where I leave you. Blakely is down to your left and Cuthbert is up to your right. Fort Gaines is straight ahead, and over to your right front is the town of Coleman, about halfway between Fort Gaines and Cuthbert on the road that goes by Cotton Hill, which ain't too far from Georgetown." The two men shook hands and parted company. Big Amaziah looked back over his shoulder from astride the big mule and yelled, "You won't forget your promise, now will you, Nelson?"

"Good-bye, my friend," Nelson called out. "I will try to see you on my way back to Albany, and I will keep you informed regarding our agreement." He rode on out the trail, westward to Fort Gaines. The flat land was changed into rolling terrain as he got closer to the Chattahoochee valley, which, with the river, separated Georgia from Alabama. After a long ride, Nelson came to a clear little brook at the foot of a steep incline, where he stopped to water the horses and to refresh himself. Another rider was coming down the hill toward him and Nelson asked, "How far is it to Fort Gaines, Sir?"

"This is your last big hill. It flattens out somewhat after this one, and about a mile farther you are on the bluff overlooking the valley. I'd say that you will be there within the hour, God willing, and the creek don't rise," the man said as they passed each other on the trail, each saying, "Good day, Sir," as they met, like ships in the night, like faceless visions in a dream. Nelson began to urge his mount a little harder, as it was getting late in the day, and the thought struck him regarding what he would do if Captain Watts and the boat were not in port at Fort Gaines. Now he was nearing the wooded crest overlooking the beautiful valley where the river and lush flatlands streched in an unbelievable panorama of beauty to the blue ridges on the horizon in Alabama. The sun was now very low, nearly ready to drop, perhaps, it seemed, into Mobile Bay to be seen by his sister and Alfred Noyes from the windows of their Waverly House Hotel. His thought strayed for a moment to Octavia Walton, now the famous Madam Le Vert, the toast of the social world on two continents. Nelson snatched his day dreams back into reality as he reached the bottom of the red clay hill and entered the streets of Fort Gaines.

Chapter 6

It looked and sounded as though the local militia must be holding its drill session in the middle of the very wide main street of the town. Nelson inquired of an old gentlemen as to the whereabouts of Captain Watts. A ramrod-straight military man heard Nelson and came over to where he stood holding the two horses. "Colonel J. E. Brown at your service, Sir," he said with a dignified bow.

"Colonel Brown, I am honored to meet you. I am Nelson Tift, lately of the Augusta Guards and now located over at Albany, Georgia, on the Flint River. I was just asking the gentleman if he knows where I can locate Captain Watts."

"Mr. Tift, I will be dismissing the troops in just a short while. If you would care to wait, I would be honored to escort you to the Dill House, which is next-door to my home. We will more than likely locate Captain Watts at the Dill House, where he stays when his ship is in port. If you will excuse me for a moment, Sir," the Colonel answered and again bowed and returned to his troops. A few minutes later Nelson heard the officer's final order of the drill when he gave his troops the "Company, Dismissed!" order. The troops "fell out," and the Colonel returned to where Nelson stood holding his mounts. "Shall we repair to the Dill House, Sir?" asked the Colonel, and they made their way up the live oak-lined street past the Globe Tavern with its shining globe at the entrance. This establishment was the most popular in southeast Georgia. Across the street was the Dill House, a big two-story frame building with two large porches running across the front of the building, one downstairs and one upstairs.

"My home is the building just across that little alley-way from the Dill House," the Colonel said as they started up the steps into the hotel. Nelson glanced over next-door and saw that Colonel Brown's home was also a two story frame building and almost as large as the public house they were now entering.

Captain Watts was surprised to see Nelson and assumed that he had come by steamer. "Why, Nelson! I did not hear the whistle of a boat coming into port. What in the world are you doing over here, anyway?"

"I did not come by steamer, Captain Watts. I rode horseback from Albany over the Hartford Trail," Nelson laughed, nudging the Colonel, who was enjoying the old Captain's bewilderment very much. But the Captain was not so nonplussed that he forgot his manners. He immediately ordered two more suppers to be served at his table. The Colonel took Nelson into a little room to wash and freshen up while their meals were being brought out to them from the kitchen. During the hearty meal the Colonel and Captain Watts took turns telling Nelson about the local history and current residents of Fort Gaines.

"Nelson, this house has eight sleeping rooms for guests, and they often feed twenty at the same time. Mrs. Dill was captured by Indians when she was a young girl. After raids, the Indians would in ignorance throw away all papers and paper money. Mr. Dill would salvage it whenever she could, until in 1822, when she escaped from her captors and swam the river above Fort Gaines, she had a fortune in paper money sewed inside her old, tattered clothing. After her marriage to General Dill, they built this great two-story building. Then they built a mercantile business, a tannery, and one of the finest harness and shoe-making businesses in the southeastern United States," Captain Watts said.

"My goodness!" said Nelson. "They must really be industrious people."

"Captain Watts neglected to tell you of the latest venture of the Dills'. They have put into operation a brick kiln and are making quality bricks. They are even now laying the foundation for a big cotton warehouse," Colonel Brown said. Nelson was introduced to each person who drifted in and out of the dining room. He found Fort Gaines to be a charming place, where the people showed more refinement and good taste than most of the other pioneers he had met in southwest Georgia. "Probably it was because these people had been here longer, and the rough edges had been somewhat polished during the passage of time," Nelson reasoned as he reflected that Fort Gaines had been sitting there on the bluff for eighteen years before he had built the first little shack in Albany. These good people here in Fort Gaines were naturally that far ahead of the settlers in the newer towns, both in possessions and convenience as well as culture.

Captain Watts was speaking again, "Fort Gaines is truly the Queen City of the Chattahoochee, Nelson. It is the most important port between Columbus and the Bay of Apalachicola as it ships cotton and other products of the residents of Georgia and Alabama. Come on, Colonel, let us take our distinguished visitor across the street to the Globe Tavern and show him about." The three men had to struggle to get up from the table—such had been the great quantities of food that the house had provided and of which they had eaten copious amounts.

Charles Suddolph was the genial host of the Globe Tavern at the corner of Washington and Carroll Streets. Suddolph had to tell Nelson his favorite "General Dill" story as he had told it to visitors to his establishment for years and years.

"Young Tift, this old Indian chief from about two-and-a-half miles north of here and across the Indian line, came to see General Dill right after they started making leather goods here and told him that he had dreamed that the General had made and given to him a most beautiful saddle for his horse. Now everyone knows that this is an old Indian superstition, so General Dill, to keep relations good between the Indians and the whites of Fort Gaines, made up a fine saddle and gave it as a present to the old chief. A few weeks later the McIntosh treaty went into effect, and a great tract of land that the General had coveted for years came closer to being available to white men. The General told the chief one evening in front of a crowd of Indians and whites that he had a dream concerning a beautiful lot of land that the chief owned that was near the big waters and Cool Creek. The chief had no choice but to give the piece of land to his friend, the General, but said afterwards, 'Me dream no more. White man dream too big'." Charles Suddolph chuckled as he left them to join some visitors who had just arrived from across the river at Franklyn.

"Who are the people that the men from across the river just sat down with?" Nelson asked.

"Oh, those are some boys from downriver along the Three Notch Trail between here and Blakely," the Colonel replied.

"Three Notch Trail? Is that an Indian name?"

"Well, in a way I guess you could say so, but it actually has to do with a trail that Andy Jackson's army engineers marked for the old General and his army to follow down to where the Chattahoochee and the Flint meet at Fort Scott. He was on his way to quiet the Red Stick Creeks and the Seminoles. The General did not get to use Three Notch Trail as he had to go by way of Fort Early on the Flint and pick up some troops there. Colonel A. P. Haynes and his detachment of Tennessee Volunteers did come down the trail to Fort Scott. Many other detachments used the road, and we have since been able to utilize it for years. That trail had been a boon to the early settlers here," the Colonel told Nelson, then added, "those men from Franklyn are sitting with the downriver boys: Grimsley, McDonald, Neves, Thigpen, Carr, Porter, and Robinson. They come into town once in a great while and 'bust Fort Gaines wide open' for awhile and then go fall in bed at the Dill House. They are kin to everybody in town. We all love them and know that youth must be served. They have never caused one minute of trouble to anyone when they come in for a little fun."

"Come on, Colonel. Let us take Nelson back and introduce him to some of the folks in the tavern," suggested Captain Watts. Nelson got up and went with his escorts to the dim rear portion of the tavern where a party of sorts was in progress. Most of the young men seemed to be about Nelson's age and stopped their laughing and talking long enough to be introduced to the newcomer from Albany, Georgia.

"Mr. Tift, we have heard of your town, and Captain Watts has had some very nice things to say about you and your town. Won't you join us for awhile?" one of the young men asked.

"No, thank you boys, not this evening. I have a few places to take Nelson, and we have business to talk over, so we cannot accept the kind invitation to join you," Captain Watts said and guided his guest towards the front of the building. Colonel Brown had a middle-aged man to introduce to Nelson. The grey-haired man advanced toward Nelson and offered his big hand as the Colonel was saying, "Mr. Nelson Tift, of Albany, please meet my old friend, William McAllister. We claim him here in Fort Gaines, but he really lives across the river at Franklyn, Alabama." The two men shook hands, and Colonel Brown added, "Bill McAllister can do more with wood than any man in these parts and has also had much to do with getting the Fort Gaines Academy into operation." Another gentleman came by, and Captain Watts introduced Nelson to Ira Cushman, a local lawyer, who shook hands and wished the young gentleman the best of luck with the new town of Albany.

On the way back to the Dill House, Nelson mentioned to Captain Watts that one of his shoes was giving him considerable trouble and pain, and he thought that a pebble had probably worked through the sole. "Don't you fret a minute, Nelson. The Dills probably have the best shoeman in the United States. Charles is his name. He is a mulatto and a freed man. Runs the cobbler shop and is head of the saddlery. When we get up to my room, give me the shoe, and I'll get it fixed for you in a trice." Upon closer inspection, it was found that not only was the last broken, but a nail had, indeed, come through the sole. The Captain went downstairs with the broken shoe, and Nelson availed himself of the opportunity to strip off his clothes and take a bath, after which he brushed his clothes, hung them neatly in a closet, and climbed between the clean sheets. It had been a long trip, hard and dirty, but he had enjoyed meeting the people along the way as well as experiencing the excitement of venturing into the unknown. He lay back and felt relaxed and good all over. He must have dozed off for a few minutes before he heard the door softly open and close again. The Captain was back with his mended show.

"Nelson, I have something I copied from an old French and Indian War Military Order of 1759. It is on the wall down in the cobbler's shop. I wrote it while Charles was fixing your shoe." He handed Nelson the piece of paper with the order written in his beautiful Spencerian hand.

"STANDING ORDERS, ROGERS RANGERS"

1. Don't forget nothing.
2. Have your musket clean as a whistle, hatchet scoured, sixty rounds powder and ball, and be ready to march at a minute's warning.
3. When you're on the march, act the way you would if you was sneaking up on a deer. See the enemy first.
4. Tell the truth about what you see and what you do. There is an army depending on us for the correct information. You can lie all you please when you tell other folks about the Rangers, but don't never lie to one of your officers.
5. Don't never take a chance you don't have to.
6. When we're on the march, we march single file, far enough apart so that one shot can't go through two men.
7. If we strike swamps, or soft ground, we spread out abreast, so it's hard to track us.
8. When we march, we keep moving til dark, so as to give the enemy the least possible chance at us.
9. When we camp, half the party stays awake while the other half sleeps.
10. If we take prisoners, we keep 'em separate til we have had time to examine them, so they can't cook up a story between them.
11. Don't never march home the same way. Take a different route so you won't be ambushed.
12. No matter whether we travel in big parties or little ones, each party has to keep a scout twenty yards ahead, twenty yards on each flank, and twenty yards in the rear, so the main body can't be surprised and wiped out.
13. Every night you'll be told where to meet if surrounded by a superior force.
14. Don't sit down to eat without posting sentries.
15. Don't sleep beyond dawn; dawn's when the French and Indians attack.
16. Don't cross a river by a regular ford.
17. If somebody's trailing you, make a circle, come back onto your own tracks and ambush the folks that aim to ambush you.
18. Don't stand up when the enemy's coming against you. Kneel down, lie down, hide behind a tree.
19. Let the enemy come til he's almost close enough to touch, then let him have it and jump out and finish him up with your hatchet.

Major Robert Rogers, 1759"

"What do you think about his advice to his troops, Nelson?"

"By golly, Captain! Some things never change and this sounds like one of them," Nelson laughed. "Seriously, Captain, this order is timeless when applied to the method of warfare they used in that war—and now, as far as that goes."

"Nelson, do you remember the pretty little girl that helped serve supper?"

"Yea, sure do!" the sleepy young man answered absently.

"Well, that little girl gave birth to a perfectly normal baby last year, and a local physician, Dr. Huser, has written a treatise on this very unusual phenomenon."

"Does the girl belong to the Dills?" asked the suddenly interested Nelson.

"She was and is the apple of Mrs. Dill's eye. I would hate to be the man responsible, if and when the General's wife finds him. However, a friend of mine told me the guilty party took off for Texas long before the baby was born." Watts sighed and turned over, then turned back to face Nelson and said, "Mr. McAllister asked me to bring you over to Franklyn to meet his family and some of the businessmen in the morning. I think you will enjoy going over to Irwin's Ferry."

"Very well, Captain," answered the now half-asleep Nelson.

The next morning it was raining. After breakfast, Nelson went to see Mr. Simonton and his partner, Buchanan, at their well-kept mecantile store. He liked both men, and when he told them he could get merchandise, delivered to the landing at Fort Gaines, twenty percent cheaper than they were now buying through regular channels, both men jumped to say "yes" to his proposition and to place their orders with him. Captain Watts and Nelson then went over to the tavern and met the north-south stage that ran through Fort Gaines on its way down to Tallahassee. Fort Gaines was also the terminous for a stage that ran across to Franklyn and from there on across Alabama to Mobile. Nelson was introduced to General William Irwin who had received his rank during the Seminole Indian War and had been given a large tract of land at Shorterville, Alabama, about four miles uphill and west of Franklyn. The General had built a fine two-story mansion on a hill overlooking the picturesque Chattahoochee valley. It was said that he could see steamboats as far as five miles below Fort Gaines and be well on his way to the ferry before the steamer could tie up at the landing. The General introduced Nelson to Mr. C. V. Morris lately of New York, who was on his way down to the ferry. Captain Watts, Nelson, and the General rode down to the river with Mr. Morris, and they crossed together.

The ride was very enjoyable and the company excellent. The little town of Franklyn was set slightly upriver across from Fort Gaines on the highest land in the vicinity.

"Most of this land over here is under water during the river's flood stage," Captain Watts told Nelson just as William McAllister joined them to introduce him to folks around the little village. There was a small hotel, a barber shop, a blacksmith shop, a cotton gin and warehouse, and two general stores that appeared to sell everything from baby supplies to coffin nails. The visitor was introduced to Messers. Harvey, Green, Renfro, Dillard, Cody, and Cannon. Later on he was introduced to some dinner guests of William McAllister's at his home. He had dinner with Howell Chitty, John Pugh, Richard Spanns, and Holms Oates. After dinner the men sat around talking. Nelson told Captain Watts that is was small wonder to him that the Captain wanted to retire from the steamboat business and be at home in Fort Gaines with his friends.

The men watched the white women and the slave women making clothing from cotton — carding, spinning, weaving, using the paddle-like carding boards with their fine wire brushes imbedded in one side. The big spinning wheels and the hand looms fascinated Nelson. He noted that most of the houses in the vicinity were of logs, one room, with candles and the light of fires in open fireplaces the only source of light. Meals were cooked over the hearth. Here, as in Albany, wood was the only fuel, and ash cakes, corn bread, sweet potatoes, roasting ears in the shuck, and barbeque were cooked well as the aroma of the burning wood added to their delicious taste. Here were no such luxuries as windows or wire screens for doors and windows. Across the river in Fort Gaines, yes, in the larger houses of the more affluent these items were found.

William McAllister showed the men a barouche that he and his two blacks had recently built, and the thought of having one exactly like it set Nelson on fire. He knew he had to have one of the beautiful vehicles and asked William if he would consider building one for him.

"Now, Mr. Tift," William said gently, "this is not my main line of endeavor. However, if you will go back to Albany and have the sawyer at your mill prepare some lumber as a friend of mine did — he sent it on the stage from Conico Courthouse — I will give you the specifications of lumber needed and the hardware that has to be ordered from Macon. When you get these things sent to me, I will build you one just like this one."

"Mr. McAllister, did I understand you to say that you have a stage that comes through here from Macon?"

"Well, not exactly. Not anymore, that is. There used to be a stage that made up at Fort Hawkins about the time Macon was being settled. It came on to Fort Gaines, crossed the river, and ran on up to Sparta, Alabama, where it terminated. There were connections in Sparta for Mobile, Huntsville, and Nashville. We could go from here to anywhere in the United States — or the world — if we had the time, the money, and a constitution rugged enough to stand the hard trip. That stage now goes to Blakely and across the Chattahoochee near there to Attaway's Store in Henry County and on up to Sparta. 'Course, it ain't far downriver from Franklyn to Attaway's Store, so you just have the hardware and the lumber sent to me at Attaway's Store." William thought for a moment and then asked, "Don't the stage come through your Albany town yet, Mr. Tift?"

"No, I'm afraid not, not just yet, but we are working on it," Nelson said regretfully, silently resolving to get busy with his letter-writing to friends in high places to do something about Albany's transportation and mail problems.

Nelson thanked Mrs. McAllister for the delicious dinner, and William walked down to the ferry with his visitors. By the time they arrived at the ferry, Nelson had made a firm commitment to get the materials together and to get them to William so that the barouche could be built. Mr. William Mumford, the postmaster of Franklyn, rode back on the ferry with them. He gave Nelson advice on how to get the best rates on shipping the buggy parts, and said, "I guess Captain Watts has heard about the men who are trying to get William McAllister interested in setting up a buggy and wagon works at Cotton Hill. I know I heard it for a fact. If it is true, I shore do wish they would consider putting it over here on this side of the river as we need some kind of a business, else my post office will be closed."

Back at the Dill House, Captain Watts said, "I heard Mumford talking about the new buggy factory. I have heard a little about it, but it is my considered opinion that it is just talk. Now, Son, we have about visited out and small-talked enough. I guess it is time we got down to the brass tacks of what we want to do about the steamboat. If you had rather, I will tell you another story about General Dill being with Andrew Jackson when they went after the Seminoles."

"No, thank you, Captain," Nelson laughed. "I have heard plenty about that around Dill House. I guess we can talk business now, if you so desire."

"Very well. First of all, I think river travel and freight will drive the stages off the roads and stop the wagon trains as well."

"How so, Captain?"

"Well, we used to have real good stage services through here — all times of day, and the hotels here and in Franklyn were full every night. Just a few years back, the stage driver was every boy's hero. The sound of the horn, the sharp crack of the whip over the leader horses, the open-mouthed worship of the little boys and girls, the quick change of horses, the fashionably dressed people from the 'outside world', the interchange of mail and passengers, another blast of the horn, the crack of the whip were familiar sights and sounds, and it was all over until the next stage arrived. Then those 'next stages' got farther and farther apart as more and more steamers came up from Apalachicola to Columbus," the Captain said sadly.

Nelson thought for a minute and then answered, "Captain, in the next decade or two, we may well see the railroad push the steamboat off the rivers."

"Do you really think so, Son?"

"Yes, Sir, I think it will be a slow process just like your stages getting farther and farther apart, but it will come. Of course, they must span the rivers and creeks with bridges that will hold the weight of iron, smoke-belching monsters," Nelson answered quietly.

"Lordy me!" said the old Captain. "It just seems like yesterday that the stage from Hartford went through Macon,

Milledgeville to Fort Perry, and here to Fort Gaines then on to Big Escambia and Pine Barren, and to Pensacola. Just think, three hundred forty-six miles for twenty-five dollars, and three round trips a week! Man, that was stagecoaching at its greatest," the old Captain said, and after a moment for further reflection continued. "Nelson, you go on and take over the "Mary Emeline"; I am getting too old for the responsibility. I will sell my stock to you at cost and you assume the debts and responsibilities. Does that meet with your approval? You can arrange payment to me to fit your convenience as I trust you more than any man I have ever known."

Nelson leaned over, patted the Captain on his shoulder and replied, "Yes, Captain. That will be fine. I will try to be prompt with my payments and even double up on them now and again when the situation permits." They made up a bill of sale and a note for the payments and went down to get a lawyer friend of Captain Watts' to look over the agreement, deed, and terms to see if they had complied with the law in drawing up the documents.

Counselor Cushman looked the papers over carefully, then looked up at Nelson and said, "Mr. Tift, these are very fine and in perfect order. You, Sir, do have a decided flair for the law."

"Why, thank you, Counselor," said Nelson blushing furiously at the praise being heaped on him by this well-known lawyer. "I do study the law upon occasion and am fascinated by just a simple reading of it; however, I read for my own satisfaction, entertainment, and edification rather than with any thoughts of ever approaching the Bar," Nelson said as he, in the presence of a learned man, unconsciously slipped back into the kind of language that his father and some of his friends deplored.

"When do you think that you will be able to get the boat to Albany?" Nelson asked the Captain later that evening as they sat out on the broad porch of the Dill House, digesting another hearty supper that had been prepared for them, and faultlessly served on the snow-white tableclothes that were Mrs. Dill's pride and joy.

"We should have the new boiler in by day after tomorrow; then I want to take the rest of the cargo up to Columbus and see what return cargo there is for here, Blakely, Columbia, and Apalachicola. I will leave anything going down to the Bay at the warehouse in Bainbridge and come on to Albany. We can re-load it on the way down to the Bay from Albany. If you are ready to make the downriver trip, you can put me off at Chattahoochee, and I will catch a steamer back here to Fort Gaines."

"Captain Watts, why don't I just go on up to Columbus with you. We can utilize the run up there as sort of a trial cruise, and I can further familiarize myself with the "Mary Emeline" under your tutelage. We could be together for the round trip to Columbus and bck here. I am sure I will then be able to handle her on to Albany."

"Why, Son, I would like that arrangement very much indeed. Maybe I can hurry the boys somewhat and get the job finished tomorrow, although I am expected to ride down to Richard Grimsley's to attend a funeral for a close friend at Pleasant Grove. Would you go with me, Nelson? It will do you good. I have rented a buggy, and Mrs. Dill will have the cooks pack us a lunch. You will meet new friends and maybe a merchant or two from Grimsley's and Blakely."

"Captain, I accept your kind offer. I will enjoy meeting the families from the river road community as well as the people who might be there from Blakely." The mosquitoes were now out in force, and the two friends decided to retire to their rooms.

The weather was perfect for the buggy ride down the old river road. The sandy little road wound around under the towering trees. Every now and then the sand was replaced by red clay, and Nelson knew these portions of the road would be nearly impassable in wet weather. He saw and was amazed at the waterfalls, many of which were being utilized for power to operate grist mills, sawmills, and cotton gins. The Captain had been right in his assumption that people from the town of Blakely and other places would attend the services. Many of the men came up and introduced themselves, saying they were from such places as Howard's Landing, Porter's Ferry, Perrywood. There were settlements with strange names like Cuba, DuBose, Jakin, Bluffton, Zetto, Coleman, Saffold, and Kolomoki. They were, as a rule, merchants who had heard that he was the founder of Albany and that he had a steamboat and was able to get supplies to merchants at quite a reasonable cost.

"What and where is this Kolomoki community that some of these folks mention, Captain?" Nelson whispered to Captain Watts when there was no one around.

"Nelson, there is a community that for some reason—unknown to anybody I know—calls itself Colomokee and the creek nearby by the same name. The great Indian mound near the creek and the village goes by the name of Kolomoki. There are many more folks in southwest Georgia who cannot read and write than are able to read and write. Many people are actually going by names other than those their mothers sent to the courthouse to be recorded. The same is true of places and things. Normally a child is ten years old before his mother finds out that his name is recorded as other than the name she gave him, or the wrong name is already cut into the stone of a grave marker, and the person lies underground for years before somebody notices that the name was spelled wrong."

"Yes, I understand. This same sort of thing is true in Charleston, Savannah, and even back in my home in Mystic, Connecticut. The thing I am most interested in at the moment is to find out exactly what Kolomoki Mound is. Everybody talks about it, but no one says what it is!"

"Oh, excuse me, I see what you mean. Well, let me see. Kolomoki is a great mound built by the old mound builders who were in this country long before the coming of the Creek Indians. It is a few miles east of here. There are several smaller burial mounds around the great one, which is seventy-five feet high, and seven hundred feet around the base. Trees several hundred years old grow out of the top of the mound, which is flat like a great stage, for which it seems to have been used. The first ten feet above ground level was used to bury the dead, and toward the creek there is an underground archway or tunnel through which the honored dead were brought to be buried. As far as can be ascertained, the ancients built these mounds with mud and their hands very much as a child makes a mud pie. The big ceremonial mound was used for the Green Corn Festival and other celebrations. Once each year the Creek families came from a wide territory to be counted in a sort of census. They came to make all new pottery from the rich clay of Colomokee Creek, and to destroy all the old pottery. They came to pay their debts and give thanks to their Maker, to make friends with their enemies, and conduct affairs of state." The Captain had spoken in an undertone, interrupting himself now and then to introduce Nelson to a person who had come into earshot.

"My word, there must have been an immense gathering of the tribes at Kolomoki. There must have been thousands," Nelson said and whistled in amazement.

"Consider this, Nelson, when the Creeks held their last big get-together at Kolomoki just prior to the time that the state began to break Early up into other counties, they held the last Green Corn Festival, and there were more Creek Indians at that festival than there were settlers in Early County. This county was sixty miles square, reached from twenty-three miles east of the Flint River on the Indian boundary line and ran south to Spanish Florida, thence with said line to the Chattahoochee River, then up said river to the Indian Boundary Line and along said line to the beginning."

"You mean there were more Indians around Kolomoki during that last festival than there were whites in the whole of southwest Georgia?"

"That's right, Nelson, because Early County was southwest Georgia at that time."

Nelson nudged the Captain and asked him what a large box-like contraption was. It stood over at the edge of the clearing.

"That is an apparatus that is used to compress cotton so that the bagging and bands can be put around it as bales are formed for easier handling and shipping. But, of course, you have brought, handled, and shipped cotton before."

"Sure have, plenty of it too, but this is the first time I have actually seen how they do it," Nelson whispered. He walked over to take a closer look. The fifteen foot "screw" looked as if it had been carved out of a good-sized log. A boom extended from it so that an animal could walk around and around, screwing the top of the cotton box down onto the cotton-filled interior until it could not be forced any farther down. Then iron bands were inserted in special slots, around the bagging, down into which the cotton had been forced. At this point, the pressure was released and the box opened. The cotton expanded immediately to secure the bands around the bale of cotton. Nelson stood and studied the procedure and the clever way in which the contraption had been devised. He made a few notes and went to join the mourners who were now filing into the big white-painted church. Nelson thought as he walked over, "I can and will build one of those compresses in Albany just as soon as I can get to it." Nelson was suddenly ashamed of himself for having selfish and irrevelant thoughts in the house of the Lord and especially at such a time when one of God's children had been called home.

Reverend R. C. Smith of Irwington, Alabama, which some called Eufaula, preached a beautiful sermon. The air was close inside the building, flies droned incessantly and the upright pews were most uncomfortable. Nelson had just begun to realize there was a pair of dirty feet somewhere near him when the minister concluded the services and beckoned for the pallbearers to come forward. They carried the flower-laden casket out the doorback to the small, but very neat, cemetery. Nelson stood beside John Sutlive who, after the brief graveside service, introduced himself to Nelson and asked him to come down to where he was building a cotton chute and a warehouse on the flats near the steamboat landing at Fort Gaines.

"I am experimenting with a chute to eliminate the back-breaking job of getting the cotton bales on board the steamers. I have a compress even better than the one I noticed you inspecting a while ago." They stood for a moment and Nelson told John that he was having much difficulty with the Albany Board Street landing in wet weather. He also told John that he had experimented with building wooden ramps but that each time, they had been swept away to high water.

"I know what you mean. That is why I am building my chute as far above the high water mark as possible," Sutlive laughed.

On the way back to Fort Gaines, Nelson asked numerous questions about the people he had met. He tried to write down the name of each. He had the names of Sheffield, Bush, Hays, Grimsley, Spann, Porter, Boles, Roe, Jones, Weaver, Brantly, Wilson, Watson, Carr, Hendrick, Floyd, Roberts, Burch, Collier, Fowler, Wood, Mercier, Dickson. He also had a few names from Cuthbert and Coleman, like Greer, Phillips, Sharp, Martin, Hawk, Strickland, Coram, Rivers, Moye, Bass, Brown, McDonald, Sands, Bailey, and Rumford. Nelson read his notes to the Captain, and the old man nearly fell out of his buggy he laughed so hard.

"Boy, you really got a bucket-full of 'em and most of them spelled right, but you have Coleman, Blakely, Franklyn, Kolomoki, Bluffton, and Cuthbert folks all mixed up with folks from the river road communities, Fort Gaines, and everywhere else. I guess that is all right; most of them are kin one way or another down in this neck of the woods."

"The trip back was made without further incident, and the Captain found out that they would be able to leave Fort Gaines the following morning. The work had been completed on the boiler.

They cast off the lines that had tied the "Mary Emeline" to the two sycamore trees at the landing and started upriver. The Captain instructed Nelson in river navigation and kept a constant running commentary on the channel, sand shoals, currents caused by shifting sandbars, and creeks like the Pataula. The Cemochechobee was the northern boundary of the Jackson treaty; above it were Cool Branch, Hitchiti, Upatoi, and others. Some of the time, they were close to the Alabama shores, and then the channel and steep banks would indicate that the channel had changed to the Georgia side.

"We call it the Alabama side and the Georgia side, but strictly speaking both shores are in Georgia. The State of Alabama boundary runs along the high-water mark on the western bank of the Chattahoochee. If one wants to get technical, that can be several miles up toward the ridge on the western banks of the river, unless, of course, there happens to be a cliff. Then the line would be wherever the high-water mark is going up the incline," the Captain told Nelson in all seriousness. Nelson knew that this was the truth but that there were little "port" villages along the river, on the Alabama side, which were frequently inundated with flood waters, yet they were still considered part of the state of Alabama.

They tied up under a steep bluff on the Alabama side. The Captain told Nelson that they were now in Irwintown and that it was the big Indian town of Eufaula before the Indian removal.

"There is a good river tavern up on the bluff, and I want to take you up there while the boys are getting some wood cut." Steps had been cut in the clay; they made their way up these steps to the tavern. This destination proved to be a large two-story building with a welcoming porch that ran all the way across the front of the house, both downstairs and upstairs. Nelson thought it a very grand building to be way out here in the middle of nowhere. Inside, the owner of the tavern shook hands with Nelson when the Captain introduced them. They were given a table toward the back of the main dining room. The Captain excused himself and hurried back to the rear dining room to speak to some people there. He came back at once and said, "Son, there is a young woman back there who says that she knows you. She is the daughter of the preacher across the river at Georgetown, and they want you to come back to their table with me."

"Captain, who are these people who say they know me?" asked Nelson, hanging back uncertainly.

"The Reverend Joshuah Mercer, brother of Jesse Mercer, President of the Georgia Baptist Convention. The young lady is Maria Mercer, who lives in Georgetown. Her father preaches at our church in Fort Gaines once in a while and that's how I came to know them. But come on, Boy, they are waiting dinner on us."

Joshuah Mercer looked about the same as when he had preached at Hawkinsville. He extended his bear-paw-like hand and said, "Nelson, I am so happy to see you. We have been hearing splendid things about you and your town over on the Flint."

Nelson would never be sure of what he had replied. Just then he turned to face Annie Maria Mercer and became further confused as she took his hand and said, "I am happy you are here, as I have been thinking about visiting some relatives at Palmyra and wanted to know more about that section around your new town of Albany. My father might even be called to preach down that way soon." There was a mischievous look in her eyes as she laughingly added so low that only he could hear, "You did not think I had forgotten you, did you, Nelson Tift?"

"Well, I should hope not, Miss Mercer!" Nelson answered while trying to gain control of his surprise and emotions. Why did this slip of a girl seem to have him on the defensive every time they met and talked? The self-posed question irritated Nelson and he resolved at once to regain his composure. Food was being served at the table, and the older people were busy trading information and perhaps a bit of gossip, leaving the field clear for the younger couple to spar a little as the young do when getting acquainted after having been separated for awhile.

"Maria, how do you like Georgetown?"

"Never you mind Georgetown. What I want to know is how things are over at Albany. Will it be a success? I don't want to get my father sent to Palmyra if you are not going to make a great success of your Albany. I wager I could make your town a success!" Maria ended on a defiant note.

Nelson tried to evade Maria's questions and pointed statements by saying, "You know, seriously speaking, I have been thinking about your Uncle William Mercer and wondering if he would consider coming to Albany and running a sawmill for us."

"Yes. Uncle William, his wife and children are at Palmyra now, and I think that he would be happy to take over your old mill. But back to me. What do you intend doing about me? Do you want me to be an old maid following my father from one little town to another until I am too old to have a home and children of my own?" Maria threw the startling question at him as if they had been talking the matter over for weeks.

"Young woman, do you go around teasing every man you meet the way you do me? If so, it is a wonder that you don't have a house full of children by several different husbands, by this time," Nelson sighed, dismayed with himself for having let the conversation get away from him again.

"Now, now, Mr. Tift. Temper, temper! No, I don't go around teasing men, and I am not teasing you. Please don't be angry with me; it just happens that I am single-minded, and as I set my heart on you to be my escort that time in Hawkinsville, I just never have been able to change it — even when you won't notice me, or when you don't make any attempt to contact me. So there, Mr. Smarty, now you know that I am a shameless hussy and that I admire you inordinately," Anna whispered fiercely. She buried her beet-red face in her hands.

Nelson was so taken aback that his blood pounded through his whole body. Just as suddenly, he felt that his body had turned to cold stone. His heart felt as if it were in his throat. He quickly rose to his feet, took Maria by the hand, and led her out on the front porch, mumbling, "You-all, please excuse us. I think that Miss Mercer is going to swoon if I don't get her out in the air for a moment."

"Never been sick a day in her life," Joshuah Mercer whispered to the Captain, who winked back when the Reverend slyly nudged him in the ribs.

Out on the porch, Maria turned to Nelson and said quietly, "I know what you are trying to do in Albany, and I know you have so much on your mind that you cannot be bothered with a silly girl like me. I want you to know that I am on your side. I am ready, willing, and able to help you in all your endeavors."

Nelson held her hands and looked deep into her eyes as he said, "Make fun of me, even ridicule me, but please don't make light of my regard for you. That wounds me deeply. Please listen to what I must say. To me you are a beauty; my mother would be extremely proud of me if she knew that a girl such as yourself could even consider sharing her life with me. My mother would be deeply disappointed if she ever found out that I had a chance with a girl like you and let you slip away. You are right about my having much responsibility thrust upon me, both by my creditors and my friends. I have them, they depend on me, they are legion, and sometimes the load is more than I can bear. I have known for some time that there had to be a someone, somewhere, such as you, to share my life—the little triumphs and the many defeats I experience as I make my way along. I have seen a few young women that I have been drawn to, but my uncertain position in life at the moment and my traveling so much of the time and my lack of information as to the young ladies' backgrounds and accomplishments tended to make me hesitate."

Little Annie Marie stood looking in disbelief at Nelson. "Oh, my!" she said. "Talk about asking for the time of day and getting a clock-making lesson for answer! You know, Nelson, you take the cake for making high-sounding speeches at the wrong time." She stood there stamping her feet in frustration at the now uncertain young man. Her father and the Captain walked out onto the porch.

Captain Watts introduced Nelson and Maria to a Mr. Sheppard whom they had met in the dining room.

"Mr. Sheppard wants to drive us down to see his newly-built Cape Cod cottage a few blocks from here. Would you and Maria care to ride down with us?" the Captain asked Nelson.

"Father, why don't you and Captain Watts go on with Mr. Sheppard? Mr. Tift and I will be fine here on the porch until you return," Annie Maria answered quickly.

After the others had gone, the two young people talked for a while with the owner of the tavern, who told them that the building had been built just the year before, but it was really the first permanent building built since the Indians left the country. He asked Nelson about the old White Horse Tavern in Connecticut and if he had ever been inside it. Nelson told him that his grandfather had taken him to the old tavern, that it had been in continuous use since 1673, but that it was in Newport, Rhode Island.

As they walked along the porch, Maria told Nelson that she had been to school at La Grange College for a short while and had enjoyed it very much. She had met some wonderful young women from many places in Georgia and Alabama. They saw Captain Watts and her father return and went to meet them at the hitching post.

"Well, Nelson, we are going to have the Reverend and his daughter with us on board the 'Mary Emeline' all the way up to Columbus. Won't that be splendid company?" the Captain said. Nelson glanced quickly at Maria, and a slight smile of understanding passed between them.

"Reverend Joshuah, will you have to go over on the ferry to Georgetown to get anything before we are ready to proceed upstream?" Nelson asked.

"No, son. We left Georgetown to come here and go by buggy to the Fort Mitchell and Phenix Girard area. We were going to cross the river at Columbus and come back by way of Lumpkin and Cuthbert. I have already notified the friend who was lending us his rig for the trip. Now all that is to be done is to board your steamboat."

"Father dreads these long buggy and wagon rides when he travels, and this trip on the steamer will be good for both of us. Oh, I know that I shall have a famous time!" Maria sang out in exultation as she gave Nelson her hand, and he led the group down the steps and aboard the "Mary Emeline." Captain Watts escorted Maria and her father to his cabin and told them that they must consider this as their quarters for the duration of the trip. The men left Maria alone in the cabin and made their way back to Nelson at the wheel. There they stood swapping stories about the river. The younger man did not mean to eavesdrop but could not help hearing their conversation.

"Reverend, it is not commonly known, but civilization came very close to being here before it came to the Savannah area. Father Juan Ocon came to the Coweat-Cusseta-Fort Mitchell area in 1679. The Franciscans came to the same area in 1681. The Savacola Mission was built where Fort Mitchell was later built and Santa Cruz de Savacola Mission was established where the Chattahoochee and the Flint meet. By 1696, Pensacola had been founded as a fort. Pensacola, of course, survived, as did Mobile and Biloxi. But the Missions on the Chattahoochee and Flint Rivers were doomed by the very Indians the Spanish were trying to convert," Captain Watts said.

"Yes, Captain. The Indians were flattered and impressed by the attention and customs of the Spanish at first, but they soon tired of the priest's stories and became restive under the iron discipline of the church. Some of the chiefs wanted more than one wife. They liked to drink the white man's whiskey, but unfortunately, they went wild with intoxication and became unmanageable. The practice of having to observe all of the church's holidays began to bore them. The Indians turned on their teachers and attacked the Missions, sometimes destroying them and killing the gentle priests. The Spanish gave up and retreated to their strongholds on the coast. Of course, Spain tried to hold the upriver trading posts that William Panton had either established or furnished with supplies. The Panton and Leslie Trading Company furnished the bulk of trade in this section we are going through now until 1802, when the constant bickering began between the Georgians and the Indians, the United States and the Indians, the Indians and the Indians. English and Spanish agents were stirring up trouble with the Indians and the early settlers. The nearly complete collapse of the Spanish dream in North America at about the same time that William Panton died stopped all civilization efforts in this section until after Horseshoe Bend. The Jackson Treaty opened up the new territory to the pioneers from Georgia, Tennessee, Alabama, and South Carolina."

Nelson was most impressed and a little surprised to hear the Reverend talk about anything other than religion and the weather. He had a question or two that had formed in his mind, but he let well enough alone and held his tongue. Captain Watts came over with an offer to pilot the "Mary Emeline" for a spell and said, "Of course. You heard us talking? I knew most of what the old boy was saying, but he seemed to enjoy talking about it; and we can always learn something about anything if we care to listen."

Nelson saw Maria up forward on the deck and went to join her. They stood together and watched the shore line slip by. The river was clear of snags and floating logs at this point, the water clean and clear. They held hands and watched the splendor of it all. Nelson could feel Maria's pulse pounding and was humbled by the very thought of this lovely girl standing beside him. The fact that this woman he now knew would be his wife some day in their future made him only dimly aware of the remainder of the trip to Columbus. He remembered her rosy lips, her ready laughter, the softness of her eyes, and the touch of her gentle hand. He knew he was falling more in love with her each time the big paddlewheel went around. The boat tied up at the Columbus landing late that evening, and Maria asked Nelson if he could get her some writing materials so that she could have a letter posted in Columbus. He went at once to get the little portable secretary from the cabin and watched as she wrote in a remarkably well-formed hand, a letter to her uncle Jesse, telling the President of the Baptist Convention of Georgia why she hoped her father could receive a call down to the Albany-Palmyra-Newton territory.

Since, of course, everyone on board knew by now that these two young people were thinking only of each other, it was of little interest to the others that Nelson and Maria sat on deck until late that night. There was a pretty half moon that seemed to float in and out of the clouds above them. The dank smell of the river was mixed with the scent of wild flowers. Nelson unburdened himself of the many little secrets that he had dared not tell even to his brother, Charles. He had anxieties about some of the trades he had made where the outcome was still uncertain. He told her of his plans, his hopes, and his dreams. Maria answered that his plans and his hopes and dreams would now be hers also and that she was willing to devote the rest of her life to helping him make them all come true and his life a little easier. It seemed like minutes later, but was, in fact, hours later, that Captain Watts came out on deck and suggested that he and Nelson make a place for themselves to sleep the rest of the night.

Later that night after Nelson had tried without success to go to sleep, he turned over for the uncountable time, and the old Captain said softly, "So this is it? Got it kinda bad, ain't cha, Boy?"

The "Mary Emeline" had been unloaded and had taken on new cargo for the downriver trip without incident. Maria and her father had walked about Columbus with Nelson until the Captain signaled with the whistle that they were ready to "cast off." They went aboard the "Mary Emeline" and Maria stood by Nelson as he piloted the steamer down toward her home in Georgetown. "Maria, why do some folks call the town across from Georgetown 'Irwintown' and others call it 'Eufaula'?"

"It was the home of the Eufaula tribe before Horseshoe Bend. After the Jackson Treaty, it was renamed 'Irwintown', but after a while the old name of Eufaula was still being used so often that it was just renamed Eufaula." They continued to talk until Captain Watts relieved Nelson at the wheel just before time to pull into the landing and let Maria and her father off at Georgetown. The next stop was at Fort Gaines to unload some cargo and take two horses aboard. Captain Watts was leaving the "Mary Emeline." Nelson had always dreaded good-byes, and these two just a few hours apart were hard for him to bear, but he managed to let the old Captain know that they would be seeing each other soon and that the Captain would have word of him meanwhile. The "Mary Emeline" was well on her way toward the Blakely-Columbia landing before he realized fully that he was now the master of the steamer; as such he would have to bring to a halt his day—dreaming and accept this great responsibility. They had cargo for several small landings before they arrived at Bainbridge on their way up the Flint to Albany. Nelson had decided to go along with the original plan of Captain Watts' and leave that cargo that was not destined for Albany at the warehouse at Bainbridge, where it could be picked up again on the way back down to Apalachicola.

Chapter 7

The "Mary Emeline" arrived at the Broad Street landing in Albany on May 10th, 1837. Nelson was elated over the success he had enjoyed as master of the "Mary Emeline," but no sooner had he docked the steamer and tied her up, than bad news met him head on. Mr. H. Atkinson was terribly upset over an alteration that had been made earlier by Nelson in plans of the town. Charles informed Nelson that Atkinson was telling one and all he was ready to sell out to the Tifts or anyone else who was interested.

"Tell Mr. Atkinson that I will meet with him just as soon as I can get some business attended to and clean up a little. Charles, tell him that I will be happy to accommodate him in this matter. Try to make him feel like I am not upset over this turn of events."

Later that day, Nelson met with Atkinson, and they came to an agreement: Atkinson would take the barges and boat at a two thousand seven hundred dollar loss to Nelson, who would assume all of the rest of their business ventures at cost, with all the responsibilities, profits, and losses. The required papers were drawn up, duly witnessed, and sent to Newton to be recorded. Nelson and Charles sat up nearly all night, and by lamplight figured their accounts to see where they stood after this large transaction and settlement with Atkinson, and full payment to Captain Watts.

The following morning Nelson left by stage for Hawkinsville and from there went to Macon where he traded for two solid weeks. He confirmed a trade with the Flint River Land Company of Macon, selling them twelve-eighteenths of the three lots of land where Albany was being settled. He reserved fifteen building lots for eight thousand dollars, at four thousand down and the balance in the script of the Flint River Land Company.

This was deposited with Rawls and King Company of Hawkinsville as collateral security, and applied to the debts of Nelson Tift. Nelson then went about getting quit-claim titles to town lots and made warranty deeds to twelve-eighteenths of land lots numbered three twenty-three and three twenty-four, and quit claim title to the like portion of three fifty-four, all in the first land district of Baker County, to the new land company.

On the evening of June 5th, 1837, Charles and Nelson had worked over their books for three hours when Charles suddenly put down his ledger and sat back.

"According to my figures, you now have twelve thousand dollars more in assets than you do in liabilities, and we can add to that the additional thirty feet of closed-in warehouse space we have completed since these figures were compiled. This will bring in more revenue."

"That sounds very impressive, Little Brother. Anything else to add to that optimistic report?" Nelson asked good-naturedly.

"Well, let me see. We have a first-rate garden over behind those false-front buildings, in the big clearing bounded by Pine, Washington, Broad, and Jackson Streets. We have the four-foot-deep canal cut four hundred feet down to the river that is saving much in time and labor, especially in wet weather. We average taking in one hundred eighty dollars a day through shipping, the store, warehouse storage, sawmills, and the sale of land," Charles paused and resumed counting off the pros and cons of the business by saying, " 'Course, there is bad news, too. You told me to take good notes if I could not get cash. All that the majority of our customers have for collateral is more land so I am not sure if it is good business for us to take any more land as security. In addition to that I have not been well since you left on your trip and have been taking some vile-tasting medicine that Doctor Meals gave me."

"Hold on! Who is this Doctor Meals that gave you the medicine?"

"Oh, he came here from his home in Micanopy, Florida. I heard that he is not a real medical doctor but has had much success with the Indians down around Micanopy. He came up on the 'Mary Emeline' from Apalachicola on her last trip and brought much 'native' medicine with him. He bought a lot here and got some lumber from our mill. He had a little two-room shack built. He is a good man, and I think he will make us a good citizen," Charles answered.

"I will have to check up on our new 'doctor' a little and see what the other physicians think about him. What kind of medicine did he prescribe?"

"He says it is 'Cinchona', which was introduced to the Indians of Florida in the early 1600's as 'Jesuit's bark' in recognition of the religious order that first used the bark of the cinchona tree to treat fever."

It had not rained for several weeks, and the river level was low. Nelson went down to Bainbridge by stage to see about some financial matters and paid off some debts that were outstanding there. He paid the boat hands in the amount of nine hundred dollars; there were some due bills for another six hundred. Peabody's note had been collected by Mr. Morgan, and Nelson collected more from other merchants, which he used wisely. He sent four hundred to Gonedy and Kimberley of Hawkinsville toward the draft for one thousand three hundred ninety-eight dollars he had made on previously deposited one thousand fifty-six dollars in cash. Nelson was very relieved to get their receipt on this latter transaction. He toyed with the idea of having some things shipped up to Albany from Bainbridge but decided not to place an order at this time because of the low water and the risk of getting his supplies either tied up on a shoal or lost, if a boat went down. He spent the night at the boarding house. Some friends sat with him on the porch, and they talked and visited until the mosquitoes drove them inside. It was little better inside except that the bedcovers could be pulled over one's body and head if one did not mind the sweat that rolled off his body and soaked into the sheets. Nelson was up bright and early and ready for the stage going north when it came through. The driver of the stage was from southeast of Tallahassee, and Nelson struck up a conversation with him to ask if he had ever heard of a Doctor Meals from down at Micanopy.

"Yes, I have heard of him, Mr. Tift. I have a cousin a-living down that away who swears that Doctor Meals is good as any regular medicine doctor. Now this cousin, several times removed, you understand, says if Meals don't think he knows what ailing ye, he'll tell ye so and try to get ye to go to a real medicine doctor."

The clouds had been gathering, and it started raining about the time they got to Blue Springs, and by the time the driver let him off at Tison's ferry just below the boat landing, it was pouring down.

It rained, and it rained, not letting up until 23 June, 1837. The river was back up, and on 27 June, 1837, a coal barge arrived from Apalachicola loaded with a consignment of goods from Asa at Key West. Now Nelson, at last, had the supplies he had promised the merchants at the towns and crossroad stores. Eight black hands from Key West came up with the barge. They were to remain in Albany at a rental to Asa of two hundred a year per head. Letters from Asa and Amos Chapman were found inside the bill of lading. Nelson put the word out to the merchants concerned that their shipments had arrived. Some of it would go out to them by boat, some by wagon, and some of the merchants would call for their shipments in their own wagons.

Nelson went down to Tison's ferry with Uncle Billy to catch some fish. Charlie Tison was on duty there. He told Nelson that he was never going to be able to get around to cutting all that timber all up on the Kinchafoonee and the Muckalee creeks unless his old man agreed with him to get rid of the ferry.

"Charlie, you tell you father that I will give him whatever he figures is fair and take the ferry off his hands. I agree with you that it is silly for you-all to run the ferry above Albany for the Tinsleys and have this one down here below Albany—this far downstream from your home—to take care of. If he wants to turn it over to me, I will tow it to just above the Broad Street landing, make it a little larger and more efficient and put it into service until the day comes when I can build a new one or even get a bridge built across the Flint."

That evening after they had returned to the store and had finished cleaning the fifteen bream and several nice bass, Uncle Billy, Charles, and Nelson enjoyed a fish fry behind the warehouse on the canal.

"Nelson, did you talk to Charlie Tison about the idea he has for the floating mill?"

"No, I did not. He was so busy talking about how he would never get around to cutting all the folks' timber who want to hire him, and how his helping run their old ferry is cutting into his time at the floating mill. What has he in mind for the floating mill? Using waterwheel to give the mill alternate power?"

"Why, how did you know, if you didn't talk about it with him?"

"If'n you'd a-asked me, I'da told ye that Brother Hawkins and Nelson done gone into all that back afore they got the little light engine for it," Uncle Billy said as he spat into the flames for emphasis.

"That is right, Little Brother. We have been down that river before and discussed the feasibility of using an alternate waterwheel even after we decided to go for the steam engine. We would just use a gear to shift from steam into water power and have the necessary pulleys, belts, and chains installed from the water wheel to the saw." He sqatted down in the light of the fire and started drawing some rough diagrams of the chassis of the mill and its saw, boiler, and furnace. He made a rough estimate of how much room was left to insert a wheel.

"Looks like from your figuring that all we need is another shaft, a simple gear, belting, and the necessary 'know how'," Charles said.

"I think you are right, Charles. There seems to be just enough room to make the modification without changing a single thing," Nelson echoed, and added, "Take Uncle Billy with you out to where Charlie Tison has the floating mill. Go out early tomorrow and get your heads together with Charlie Tison and see what you need to get the job done. I don't want either of you ever to tell Charlie that it is not his original idea."

Everyone was getting excited over the plans for the Fourth of July celebration many days before that glorious date arrived. People were coming in from all over the countryside. There was to be a barbecue. Nelson had written a speech and was going to give it. Of great interest there was a big dance planned; many said it would be the first public dance in Baker County. The town was a beehive of activity until the great day arrived. Nelson made his short, patriotic speech near the limestone-sink pond at the corner of Jackson and Broad, an unsightly place in dry weather, but when filled with beautiful blue-green water, a most delightful spot for an outing. After extolling to the crowd the heroics of their fathers and grandfathers who had paid the price for their beloved country with toil, agony, and daring, he reminded them of the shortness of time a human being has on this earth. He earnestly urged the present generation to try to leave southwest Georgia in good condition for those who would follow, telling them in closing, "Jesus had many things to accomplish in a relatively short life on this earth, but none compared with the purchase of man's redemption—with his own life. The Christ showed us, in human terms, what God is like, and what God thinks of man. He told us in veiled language what heaven is like and how to experience heaven to some degree while we still abide on earth. Jesus shows us our shortcomings in spiritual things and how to grow into the person He calls us to be. One thing dwarfs all that our Saviour does for us. He purchased our redemption with His own innocent life." Nelson paused, cleared his throat, and added, "My friends, I feel sadly inadequate when I try to speak of such things. All of us here in the wilderness feel close to our Maker for we should surely perish here without His guidance, mercy, and the bountiful flow of provender from His fields, streams, and forests. These good things that He so freely gives us must be cherished and passed on to our children a little better than we found them."

    The Fourth of July barbecue was a giant affair, with the women setting the tables especially built for the occasion with the most cherished secrets from pantries and shelves. Pies and cakes and breads and fixings for the pork and two beeves that had been slowly turning on their hand-operated "spits" all during the night. The busy women traded gossip as they worked; the small boys and girls ran up and down and around and around, laughing and yelling at the top of their shrill little voices. The young folk either openly courted, played coy, or made a point of ignoring each other in public to show that they did not really care. The men talked politics, and there were endless comparisons of the former President with the new one. Everyone in southwest Georgia was standing firm behind "Old Hickory" over the new President, Martin Van Buren, the eighth president of the United States. They discussed the crops, the river, roads, and bridges, the newly inaugurated Eastern Pony Express that was going to transport mail a hundred miles in one day in those sections of the country that would be fortunate enough to get on one of the routes. All of these were the topics of conversation. Nelson was amazed to find many people who were not able to read or write—except to sign their names a little—but who could somehow quote lengthy passages from the Bible. No matter what topic was being discussed, one of these old-timers could instantly quote something from the Bible that either set a precedent for what was being said or drew a parallel with the subject.

They danced all night, or until the fiddlers wore out their strings with their bows or the toes of their shoes with their stamping and keeping time to the lively music. Some of the music and words were light and gay, some of them had a tinge of sadness.

"In my dreams by the stream last night I wandered, and I thought my love was standing at my side / Once again then I told her I loved her, Once again she promised to be my bride / And as I turned to kiss her, I awakened / I called her, but she was not there to hear / My heart lies buried with her 'neath the willow / In that old Savannah home I loved so dear."

A great white line was drawn down the middle of the dance floor and when a young woman dancer grew tired, she went to the women's side of the line and rested. Even some of the older men retired to their side of the line for much needed rest from time to time. News of the great celebration's success spread over the countryside and did wonders for the reputation of the struggling little town of Albany. Little snatches of conversation could be heard throughout southwest Georgia, "Oh, did you hear what Mamie wore at the Fourth of July celebration and dance at Albany? She said there were several costumes in the crowd that made hers look old-fashioned" . . . or if one happened to be listening to small talk in one of the saloons or other meeting places of menfolk, he might have heard comments like, "Well, as Squire Walters was saying over at Albany last week when I was over there placing an order for a new steammill . . . " Slowly but surely the reputation of the little town grew and it began to burgeon as the center of activity and trade for southwest Georgia.

Nelson took the stage to Hawkinsville where he was able to pay a draft for Tift-Atkinson in the amount of one thousand four hundred dollars. He wanted to go on to Macon, but there was not a stage until the next day. Rather than lose a full day, he purchased a sturdy-looking mare and was nearly ten miles down the road before he realized he had been sold a blind animal. But the mare was a well-trained mount, gentle, patient, and strong. Nelson rode her on into Macon without incident. Upon arrival in Macon, Nelson went directly to see Alexander Shotwell, and they immediately immersed themselves in a long-planned transaction: Shotwell wanted to enter into large-scale merchandising at Albany and gave Nelson two hundred fifty dollars to bind the deal until they could consummate same. Nelson sent the two hundred fifty dollars to LaFitte in Charleston. This came very near to closing out this account of long standing. Nelson sold the blind mare as a blind mare that had brought him without incident from Hawkinsville to Macon, and did not lose anything on the transaction.

When Nelson arrived home on the stage, he found that his new overseer, A. L. Sellers, had finished up the twenty-by-four-foot boat tht Nelson had designed and asked him to build. They took four black hands and filled the boat with five hundred pounds of bacon. On 30 July, 1837, they started out for Reaton's shoals. As they passed between an island and the shore, one of the hands, contrary to Nelson's orders, stood up in the boat. This action turned the boat sidewise in the swift current and put them in danger of being swamped, filling, and capsizing. Nelson knew that the best remedy in this instance was to order the boat headed into the swift water, but just before they had gotten into the predicament, one of the hands had pointed out a fifteen-foot alligator over on the island sunning himself. They would just have to take their chances with the 'gator. Nelson gave the order to swing around and head the boat in to the island. Two of the hands saw they were headed right at the big 'gator which had become wide awake and was now headed straight for the water — and them. The two, again contrary to orders, stood up in the narrow beam longboat and attempted to paddle. The boat began to take on water, and

Nelson yelled, "Everyone that can swim get into the water; those who can't swim, hang onto the boat." But once again, against orders, the panic-stricken blacks all left the boat, leaving only Nelson and his assistant, Sellers, in the now-sinking boat. One of the blacks, who could not swim, was saved by Nelson who threw him a paddle and instructed him to hang onto it. This man was out in deeper water than the others, in real trouble, and he was beyond taking advice. He started pawing the water in panic. Nelson swam quickly to him, but the poor fellow tried to drown them both. Nelson struck back and even cursed the man in an attempt to shock him into some semblance of sanity. This seemed to work as Nelson started slowly pulling the black toward the shore, talking soothingly to him as they got closer to the shallow water.

"Now if you want to be saved, you must stop acting like a baby," Nelson said softly over and over, and it seemed to produce the desired effect, as the man appeared to be calming down somewhat.

Just when it seemed that the battle was won, the man suddenly went berserk and attempted to drown Nelson, who went under water and surged upwards again getting under the crazed man and breaking loose before the big man could strangle him. Sellers got to them just in time to help subdue the mad fellow. Everyone calmed down, and they got the overturned boat floating again. The Negro, Ben, was never able to remember the incident although his friends, who had seen it, told him the story many times. Ben became inseparable from Nelson Tift after that day because of Nelson's having saved his life.

They worked the boat around and got it over to the east side of the river where they tried to salvage some of their cargo, which, when dried out, would be all right. Nelson left the men with A. C. Sellers and trudged back toward home. He was nearly there when one of the blacks came running to report that one of John Montgomery's blacks had drowned and had not been missed in all the excitement.

Sale of town lots had been brisk during the first part of 1838 in Albany, and on the first day of March Nelson entered into an agreement with Alexander Shotwell to get into the mercantile business in an expanded degree. Nelson was to furnish six thousand dollars to found the business, two thousand in merchandise, the store they would operate from, and the use of his warehouse. Shotwell came up short of the money he had agreed to furnish and contributed only two thousand in cash to get the business started. Charles and Nelson were already committed to build a two-story brick building for a store and a house, and were cutting the timbers for the county to complete two bridges over creeks just north of Albany. The Inferior Court had just given the order to build five roads leading into Albany and things were indeed looking up for the fledgling frontier town.

The news that a magistrate's court would now be held at regular intervals in Albany was a big step forward, as all the running back and forth to Newton to go to court had been expensive and time-consuming. The distance and condition of the road had made it necessary to spend at least one night at the county seat when there on business. This, of course, entailed the spending of a night at a hotel or a boarding house, and the livery stable was used to care for a horse or horses for the night.

Shotwell said that he was sure that the steamboat, "Edwin Forest" was going up for sale at a reasonable price. Nelson had been waiting for a chance to get a good boat, so they decided to make an offer for the steamboat. Alexander Shotwell made a trip out of Albany for two days, and when he returned, he had the necessary backing to start negotiations to buy the "Edwin Forest." A reliable source at Milledgeville was reputed to have alleged that the Governor advanced Shotwell money on this venture, but as every ex-governor in the state was called Governor as long as he lived, it could have been Gilmer, Lumpkin, or Governor William Schley. At any rate, Tift and Shotwell would pay one-half and Cowart would pay the other half. A Captain Holland was bringing the "Edwin Forest" up to Albany from Apalachicola, and Nelson made his plans to make the downriver run to the Bay for supplies. He and Charles held a conference to see how much cash they could raise to pay for the purchases he would make at Apalachicola.

"I have exactly two thousand dollars that is not earmarked for anything and that we can spend for supplies," Charles told his older brother after making some quick calculations.

"That should be sufficient. Say, have you heard anything around here about this Captain Holland that is bringing the steamer upriver?"

"No, nothing. How about Alexander; does he know the Captain?" Charles answered and asked at the same time.

"No, I am sure that he does not, because when he came to tell me that the 'Edwin Forest' was leaving Apalachicola for delivery here, he just remarked that 'Captain Holland would bring her upriver'."

The "Edwin Forest" proved to be a larger boat than the "Mary Emeline" and was not quite as old. Captain Holland was a man of middle age who told Nelson that he wanted to go to the Tampa Bay area on some business when they got back to Apalachicola. If Tift, Shotwell, and Cowart wanted him to continue as master of the steamer, he would come back from his trip to south Florida and resume command.

The trip down to the Bay was made without any outstanding incidents. Captain Holland was a skillful pilot, not quite as familiar with the Flint as old Captain Watts but a most competent steamboat man. Captain Holland left for Tampa as soon as possible after he got the boat safely into Apalachicola. Nelson purchased his goods, picked up more that awaited him from Key West and loaded some two thousand three hundred pounds for upriver delivery. Nelson was now in full command with the consent of all concerned. The "Edwin Forest" arrived at Bainbridge in four days and remained in port there two days and then proceeded on to Albany on the twelfth day after leaving the Bay. Taking into consideration the fact that two boilers had burst and the two barges had been brought back, this was very good time.

While the boilers were being repaired at the landing in Albany, Nelson went upstream to Danville in a small boat and purchased a Negro boy by the name of Henry for nine hundred twenty-five dollars. Cowart paid half the price, as this boy was experienced in working on steamboats with cotton boxes.

On 10 April, 1838, Nelson bought a cotton box and took it to Danville where cargo from a stranded barge was loaded into it. The river was not at flood stage, but the waters were high enough for the "Edwin Forest" to make the trip; however, on the return trip to Albany, her stack hit an overhanging limb and fell off into the water. The men brought the smoke stack up from deep water, and they made the necessary repairs before negotiating the intricate shoals between their location and the landing at Albany. Nelson was so exasperated that he came very near swearing as he told A. C. Sellers, "Thunder and tarnation, A. C.! I thought surely with the high water we would not have this much trouble getting to Danville and back. I tell you that even though I respect and admire brother Glover, I won't attempt this again, even for him."

But there was to be more of the same, as they stuck three times on shoals between Pindertown and Albany before they arrived at the Broad Street landing two days later. Charles was waiting at the landing with more bad news: the barge which they had unloaded and left floating free had now lodged itself on a shoal at Philema. "Get me a change of horses and a wagon and team for A. C. and the 'hands'. We will go right on back up there and see what can be done to get her off," Nelson instructed Charles.

"I thought that you took all the cotton off the barge, so that it would float on down here, Nelson. I don't understand how it got stuck again with no more bales of cotton on it."

"You are partially right in the assumption that we took the cotton off her, but we had only about half the cotton off when we saw that she was going to float off the shoal. Our steamer and the cotton box were getting a little low in the water to make the return trip, and we had to take a chance. I am not foolish enough to take the steamer back up into that mess. That barge has about one hundred bales of cotton left on her at Philema, and we are going to have to pull her off — or over — those shoals even if we have to unload a few bales and reload them when we get her afloat again. Charles, we have to get this shipment down to Apalachicola. We should have left two days ago."

After hours of back-breaking work, and after using every trick they had ever heard of, they finally worked the barge off the shoal and got it floating.

"We should never use anything but cotton boxes anyway. If I have my way, that is going to be the way we get cotton down to Albany from now on," Nelson told Sellers, who mumbled something under his breath. "What did you say, A. C.?"

"I said I told you a way back yonder that we ought to use cotton boxes up here in this mess," A. C. said softly.

"Well, from now on, please speak a little louder, and I will listen a little closer," Nelson said gently and in a more resigned tone. "A. C., take all but one 'hand'; surely with the 'hands' that are already on the barge, you can get her down to the landing. I will follow you as closely as I can with the wagon and team and my two horses and can help pull you off if the barge goes on another shoal." Nelson followed the progress of A. C. and his men as closely as possible, at times leaving the "hand" with the wagon and horses long enough to ride through rough places to try to determine whether the barge had made it to that point. It was touch-and-go at Tinsley's ferry, but Charlie Tison happened to be on duty when the barge was about to pass through the rocks and shoals where the Muckafoonee and the Flint meet. He proved invaluable in helping guide them through these rough places.

The downriver trip to Apalachicola was made without incident, and Nelson made inquiries around the city for Captain Holland. He was not in town, and there had been no word from him at the hotel. Nelson left the now-loaded barges with Sellers and made the coastwise voyage to St. Joseph to pick up some more freight. He enjoyed another sea bath, but this time without all the fripperies that he and his friends had enjoyed the memorable evening of the bath house, the girls, and all the laughter.

Back at Apalachicola there had still been no word from Captain Holland. After talking the situation over with A. C. Sellers, Nelson decided that they would wait one more day for the now long-overdue Captain Holland. He checked into the hotel and enjoyed a hot bath for twenty-five cents, a town shave for ten cents, and purchased a much needed tooth brush for twenty-five cents. After completing his toilet, he walked around the city making notes of the retail prices so that he would be better informed as to what the "outside" merchants were charging for goods. He noted that a gallon of whiskey was one dollar, a Dutch oven was one dollar seventy-five cents — and it looked cheaply made he thought. Coffee was priced at eight pounds for a dollar; a chamber pot was thirty-eight cents; six pounds of sugar was ninety-five cents; three pounds of castile soap was seventy-five cents; twelve pounds of salted pork was one dollar. A barrel of flour sold for seven dollars; eight pounds of potash was one dollar seventy-five cents; a spindle-head was fifty cents. One large round of cheese brought three dollars, a pair of plain boots cost one dollar fifty cents; three oranges went for fifteen cents. A doll was priced at ten cents; cigars were five cents; a cowhide was ten cents; a ride on the ferry across a very wide body of water required twenty cents for a man and his animal.

During the night, Nelson slept uneasily. He thought he heard sounds around his room, and a quartet of drunks were serenading someone in the street until after midnight, when he finally fell asleep. The next morning he was infuriated at the discovery that his wallet with four hundred dollars had been taken from his trouser pocket. He notified the hotel authorities and the police, but all to no avail. The "Edwin Forest" left for the upriver run with a poorer Nelson still in command and no word from the missing Captain Holland.

The "Edwin Forest" made the run to Albany in ten days with the two loaded barges in tow. The run was easy. The boat was tied up, and the crew went ashore to cut wood for the boilers. On the twelfth of April, 1838, the waters at Reaton's shoals, though low, had been passable, and the boat safely arrived in Albany. Bad news in the form of a letter from Brother Hawkins' sister at Argyle Island, telling of her brother's passing, greeted Nelson as soon as he brought the steamer into the landing. The old man had gone to his favorite fishing hole late one evening, and when he did not return home for his supper, a boy was sent down to see whether he was all right. The boy hurried back with the shocking news that Brother Hawkins had passed away with a fishing pole in his hands, sitting with his back to the bole of a sycamore tree. The sister reported that her brother had been "porely" when he had arrived home but had recovered from the hard stagecoach ride, began feeling much better, and was soon his old self. She further stated in her letter that her brother spoke with love and affection of "his boys" as if they were really his sons and that Brother Hawkins had been given a Christian burial on Argyle Island.

"How old was Brother Hawkins, Nelson?" Charles asked after some thought.

"You know, Brother, I really do not know for sure. It is hard to tell in cases where a man retains his physical strength right up until the end, as Brother Hawkins did. I would say he was fifty-five or sixty," Nelson answered. He cleared his throat of a tightness that refused to loosen. He wiped the tears from his eyes and shook his head, "Lordy, we are sure going to miss him. He just made everything right when things were going wrong. It seemed to me that he was about the only person I ever knew who could gently scold me for my impatience or slow me down when I wanted to rush into something without first thinking it through carefully," Charles sighed.

"Aw, Charles, you just don't know the half of it. Why, when I was still wet behind the ears, he had to nurse me along. You and I must sit down and compose a letter to his sister," Nelson paused for a moment and added, "I have just learned that Mr. Mercer, who used to run the big steam sawmill over at Hawkinsville has moved out near Palmyra. You know, he is so much like our dear departed Brother Hawkins. We need him here to take over the big sawmill. I think that we should exert every effort in that direction."

"Oh, yes, I do remember Mr. Mercer and that pert little niece of his with whom we sat at the preaching that night in the new store at Hawkinsville. I hope Mr. Mercer can come here to work with us, and I surely would not mind if I laid eyes on his niece again. By the way, you did not hear whether she and her father were also out at Palmyra, did you?" asked Charles.

"Well, you can never tell. It is such a small world in some ways, but I am almost sure that Miss Mercer is not in Palmyra at the moment," Nelson said evasively but not really untruthfully. It made no difference; his statement went in one ear and out the other of his brother who already had something else on his mind to ask Nelson in regard to the upriver run from Apalachicola.

"Say, Nelson. Did you see that cotton box Mr. Glover built for us anywhere on the river?"

"Forgot to tell you, that is a real good-looking box. We saw it below Bainbridge, and the boys were in full control. How many bales did you have in that box, anyway?"

Charles reached into the pile of papers on his desk and came out with his copy of the bill of lading which he read, "Three hundred sixty-two bales at two dollars and a half with three dollars freight per bale." Charles thought a moment and asked, "That is pretty good considering what we paid Glover to build it, wouldn't you say?"

"It is, except for one item, Charles."

"And what might that be?"

"Well, you know that we are getting ready to lay the barges up for the low water season or maybe until next cotton season, and we get only the one trip from each cotton box anyway, no matter how well it is built. We might have to foot the bill for the three hands and their supervisor to stay at Apalachicola until we get them back up here. So you see 'all that glitters is not gold' in this instance," Nelson said with a sigh.

The following morning Nelson took the buggy and went up to Palmyra. He stopped at Indian Springs and bathed in the "Chief's Hole," a rectangular, deep depression seemingly cut from the living rock. A beautiful little spring bubbled up, made a pool of water about fifteen feet wide and thirty feet long, then disappeared underground only to emerge again in the form of a powerfully stimulating whirlpool of icy water in the "Chief's Hole" where it swished around and then mysteriously disappeared again for three hundred yards before surfacing in a blue boil of water similar to the "Blue Hole" over at Byron. The stream of water from this "boil" flowed to the Kinchafoonee Creek and, of course, eventually became part of the Flint River. After drying in the sun, Nelson put his trousers and jumper back on and resumed his trip to Palmyra, which was just two miles farther up the road.

Palmyra seemed to have more houses in it than did Albany, but fewer business houses. Nelson stopped at the first little wooden store he reached and went inside to inquire for his friend, Mr. Mercer.

"Well, Sir, I am Harmon Mercer. What Mercer be you seeking? May I be so bold as to inquire? The sawmill-and-gristmill Mercer; the doctor; or the preacher? They all be nephews of mine," the big man said, taking Nelson's hand into his and shaking it.

"Mr. Mercer, I am Nelson Tift from Albany, and I am looking for William, the one you describe as the sawmill-and-gristmill Mercer. Can you tell me where I might find him?"

"I'll say I can, young man. That is quite a town you are building over on the Flint, and if we don't watch our knitting here in Palmyra, I do believe that you will soon outstrip us in both size and importance. Come on; I will escort you up to the hosue," Harmon Mercer said and led the way out of the darkness of his store into the bright sunlight. They made their way up to the big house on the hill, and a familiar figure got up from the porch to meet them.

Brother William Mercer looked exactly like Nelson had remembered him. He was, perhaps, a shade thicker through the middle. They shook hands warmly, and Nelson came right to the point. He told of the loss of his dear friend, Hawkins, and explained that he needed Brother Mercer to run the sawmill and install a first-class gristmill for him.

"You people over at Albany are really building a big town. I would like very much to have a part in that work. When would you want me to come over and get started? You know, we are having company coming in here pretty quick; in fact, it's tomorrow that the company is coming, is it not, Uncle Harmon?" Brother Mercer asked.

"Yep, from what Joshuah's letter said, they will be here from Cuthbert, where he posted the letter, by nightfall this evening," John answered.

Nelson took Brother Mercer by the arm and led him out of earshot as though they were going to talk business. He asked, "Is Maria with her father?"

"Well, I'll be hornswoggled, Nelson! So that is it! I told you in Hawkinsville she done set her cap for you. Well, if that don't beat all! I wondered why Joshuah was leaving a place like Georgetown to come and look around over here. The word we got is that he thought he might get 'called' over this way. I told Uncle Harmon that Maria was behind this visit. 'Course she is with Joshuah." Brother Mercer finished with a hearty laugh, slapped Nelson on the back, and added, "You had better run, Boy, and I'll come on down and take over after I visit with Joshuah and Maria a little."

"Brother Mercer, listen closely to me. This is serious business. When Maria gets here, you get her off to the side and tell her that I have been here. Tell her you are moving to Albany to take over part of our organization and that I will be back up here to get her the day after tomorrow. I will make all arrangements at Albany for our wedding, and I want her father to come with her to perform the ceremony. Now let's go back down to the store so I can meet some of the citizens of Palmyra. Please don't say one word about the wedding until you talk to Maria," Nelson asked earnestly. They went back to the steps to tell Uncle John and his wife that Nelson was going to have to be leaving in order to get back to Albany before dark.

"It was nice talking with you, young Tift, and we hope that you will come back often," Uncle Harmon Mercer said from behind the picket fence in his yard as Nelson went back down the hill to the cluster of buildings where he met Leonidas Jordan, reputed to be one of the richest men in these parts. Also in town were Charles Randall, John B. Gilbert, Lott Warren, the Reverend Jonothan Davis, George S. Oglesby, Burch M. Roberts, Doctor Jeremiah Hillsman, and John Woolbright. After visiting all four of the general stores in Palmyra, Nelson dropped into the barber shop for a quick "town" shave and here met some more of the citizens. It rained as he was leaving Palmyra, but he drove on and soon emerged from the small shower. The rest of the drive back into Albany was made with ease. He was even able to stop two or three times and hold conversations with farmers who were working near the road. Most of the time, he just sat back and let the horse have his head and follow the little road. Nelson let his mind rove as hundreds of thoughts crowded through his head: What if Maria decided to reject him and make him a laughing stock to his friends? What if she had just been teasing him over there on the Chattahoochee River? What if she was paying him back for being so "stiff necked," as she called it? The buggy came to a halt, and Nelson jerked himself back into reality from his daydreams. He was at the corner of Jefferson and Pine Streets, and the horse had paused simply because he had a choice of whether to go east on Pine, west on Pine, continue south on Jefferson, or turn around and go back where he had been.

Later that evening, after they had eaten and were walking around seeing who was building what and where, Charles asked, "Is Brother Mercer going to be with us? How big is Palmyra? Do you reckon we can do any business with the merchants out there?

Nelson walked on a few more steps without answering and then said, "Yes, he will be down here in a few days to take over the mill and to build a grist mill. But we have plenty to do before I go up to Palmyra the day after tomorrow and bring Annie Maria and her father here for our wedding."

"You are going to do what, with whom, when?" Charles asked in amazement but trying to control his voice.

"Charles, I had dinner with Annie Maria and Reverend Joshuah Mercer at a tavern over at Eufaula, Alabama, and both of them went on the 'Mary Emeline' to Columbus and back to Georgetown with us. I think that it is time for me to get married, and I think that Maria is the right wife for me. Granted that I did not think her the most beautiful girl in the world at first, but she is, in my estimation, such a girl that will always command my esteem by her good qualities and as for her qualities of beauty, they grow with each passing day, and I am satisfied. I shall write to Mother Hannah and our brothers and sisters tonight. I must also get off a letter to Augusta for publication."

"Mother Hannah always said that 'Pretty is as pretty does'," Charles said, "and I think that Maria is head and shoulders above any girl, anywhere, in wit, charm, intelligence, and goodness. I shall be very proud to have her as my sister-in-law. I tell you, Nelson, she is the one ingredient that has been missing from our formula for success."

"I hoped and prayed that you would agree with me on this decision and that you would feel that Maria is the girl for me. Thank you, my brother," Nelson said humbly.

"You know, I don't think that I have ever heard you say the word 'love' in connection with a girl. You do, of course, love Annie Maria?"

"Yes, of course! I assure you that I do have great regard for her. She is going to be Mrs. Nelson Tift, you know. I am strongly drawn to her, and I can feel her reaching out to me. I want to share my thoughts and my life with her. You know that I have never been one to go about making public utterances about ladies or my 'love' for this one or that. Maria knows all this, and perhaps one day I shall learn more about this consuming emotion the poets and romanticists call love," Nelson finished lamely.

"Come on. Let us go to the new house. I will start getting everything ship-shape while you get the letters written," Charles proposed with a laugh and they started back toward the house.

When he was about two miles from Palmyra, Nelson saw one of the men that he had met at Palmyra.

"Hello, Mr. Tift," the man said with a sly grin. "Heard that you are about to marry up with one of old Harmon Mercer's folks. I have met the young lady, and I must commend you on your excellent taste." Nelson tipped his hat and smiled a thin little smile. He felt the red mount in his cheeks and on the back of his neck, as he urged his mount forward.

Maria was waiting with the others at Harmon Mercer's sprawling farmhouse. She was radiant, and Nelson noted that she had changed her hair style to that being worn currently by the young ladies of fashion. It became her. Nelson also noted that her dress did not seem to be as bulky and unbecoming as before. Once again he noted that she was a rather pretty young woman. With a little more skill and the right clothes, she would be beautiful. Maria and Nelson drove back to Albany together while Reverend Joshuah and his wife followed in another buggy. As they drove along, Nelson attempted to tease Maria a little about the changes that she had made in her appearance.

"I hope I have not offended my parents. The girls at college showed me that I looked so much better with just a few minor adjustments of my hair, my eyebrows and my dress. I saw the pained look my father gave me and the anxious look on Mother's face. She was so afraid that Father would make a sudden outburst," Maria explained.

"Did Reverend, er, uh, I mean your Father, scold you, Maria?"

"He opened his mouth to scold me, and I closed my eyes and prayed. Nothing happened, so I opened them, and there he was just standing there with a defeated little smile on his face and his arms outstretched to me. When I went to receive his embrace, he whispered that he was happy that I was not still hiding my beauty and my goodness under old-fashioned styles and prejudices."

"Do you know that the way your mother had you dress certainly misled me?" Nelson teased slyly.

"Why, what do you mean, Mr. Tift?"

"I mean that the first time I saw you, I thought that you were Father's little girl and that you set yourself up as one of those 'Holier-than-Thou' types with a talent for making me feel frustrated and useless," Nelson laughingly answered.

"And the next time, Mr. Tift? What did you think of me the next time you saw me at the tavern in Eufaula?"

"Well, let me see. How do you church people put it? 'A froward or a forward woman with no shame.' I think that would be estimate for you that day," Nelson said and hit the horse lightly with the whip. "Giddyap, Hoss, let's go home now."

"Mr. Tift, with all due respect to your undetermined number of hours at that great seat of learning called Yale, I, although a girl with one year at La Grange College, must inform you the word 'froward' means disobedient, intractable, or perverse. 'Forward', used as you indicated, means immodest, imprudent, eager, hasty, and worse things we won't discuss at this time. Which interpretation of your remarks must I take?" Maria quickly replied as she goaded the now unhappy young bachelor whose last moments of freedom were fleeting away.

"Well, Maria, somewhere in between the two, I guess. You know you did ask my opinion," Nelson stated a little sheepishly.

"Mr. Tift, if I had waited for you to 'pop' the question or to even think of the matter, we would not be within hours of getting married, and I would be still a preacher's daughter dependent on Christian handouts, hand-me-down clothing, and still waiting for some good man to come along and see the real me down underneath those old ill-fitting dresses. I would be forever with my hands folded like a good little girl and my face always hidden under one of those stupid poke bonnets." Maria plainly resented the way every circuit rider's daughter had to live.

"My dear," Nelson said this time with deep feeling, "that is all behind you and for the rest of our lives, we can look back on this ride from Palmyra to Albany to be married. We can remember the first time that I met you at the preaching at Hawkinsville, and the wonderful hours at the tavern in Eufaula and on the trip to Columbus on the 'Mary Emeline.' We shall recall, not only with tenderness, but with laughter and thankfulness that we two — out of all the people in the world — found each other."

"You just hush sweet-talking me, Nelson, or I will be one of those tearful brides that I detest with a passion!" Maria laughed, showing that she was once more her usual good-natured self.

Everything in the part brick-part frame Tift house was as ready for the wedding as Charles, his men, and some women volunteers could possibly make it. Mrs. John Gilbert, the wife of Doctor Gilbert, had come over from their home near Palmyra and had helped Charles do those little "extras" that mean so much on a special occasion. The good doctor had visited around town and introduced himself to the people while waiting for his wife, and the arrival in Albany of the wedding principals.

At last Nelson and Maria stood before her father, at the Tift home in Albany, Georgia. It was the tenth of May, 1838. In a few short minutes, the young couple would be made one. Mrs. Joshuah Mercer, Dr. and Mrs. Gilbert, Mr. and Mrs. Jeremiah Walters, the newly arrived John Jackson, Charlie Tison, A. C. Sellers, Mr. and Mrs. Sutton, Uncle Billy, and the faithful Ben all stood silently and respectfully as the marriage ceremony was performed. After the wedding those who had to get home before dark took their leave while the others stayed and sampled good cheer from the numerous festive bowls.

Brother William Mercer came to take over the sawmill and to build a grist mill. Mrs. Mercer and the two boys came with them. They went to work right away building the grist mill and a house for themselves on the same property. Nelson put A. C. Sellers, Uncle Billy, and three hands to work on the building program and had a place before nightfall where Mrs. Mercer could put her things out of the weather as well as a place for themselves the first night. Everything they needed to build the grist mill including the grinding stones had been ordered in advance and was waiting to be installed. Timbers had already been cut for the foundations and the other lumber laid by.

Uncle Billy hit it right off with Brother Mercer and within two weeks the whole project was completed. They decided to keep the usual one-eighth of the meal as toll for having ground the corn for the farmers. Both the stationary steam mill and the floating sawmill were working to full capacity. Two more heavy wagons, with big oxen to pull them, had been purchsed to deliver lumber. Two huge carts with oversized wheels had also been acquired to carry and "snake" logs from the forest.

Orders for bridge timbers from individuals and the County were in demand as were the standard two-by-fours used in building homes and business houses. Standard sheeting was cut by the thousands of feet: one inch thick, five to twenty-five inches wide, and in eight, ten, and twelve-foot lengths. Oak shingles were being used for all the buildings and several families made good livings my making these "shakes" from white oak. They used a long "horse"-looking contraption that the man pulling the "knife" sat on as if sitting on a horse. Making shingles looked very easy until one who was not versed in the procedure tried it.

A young "drummer" talked with Nelson at Apalachicola about a new type of roofing his company was preparing to market. It was metal, made into eight-foot-by-four-foot rectangles. The metal was easy to bend and could be cut with tinners' shears or penetrated with a nail. It was called "tin roofing." It usually had a crimped edge that fitted over another crimped edge of the panel next to it. Nelson inquired about price, wholesale (jobber) price, shipping charges, and other particulars and told the young "drummer" to have an order of it shipped to Apalachicola. From there they would take it upriver to Albany to see if the builders would buy it.

Chapter 8

On the evening of the eighteenth of May, 1838, the newlyweds went to the wedding of H. B. Gunnelson to Miss Mary Mallory. They attended the event with their friends, Mr. and Mrs. W. J. Sutton. After the simple ceremony, they returned home in the carriage. As they neared Jackson Street, Mrs. Sutton said, "Do you realize that there have been four weddings in Albany within the last ten days, and there is no place here to buy even a simple wedding present?"

Mr. Sutton was sitting shoulder to shoulder with Nelson. He felt more than saw him react to this statement, and said softly, "There will be shortly if I know Nelson Tift!"

Nelson laughed and said lightly, "Oh, no! That is Maria's department as I defer to her taste and exquisite judgement in things of this nature. It is an interesting suggestion which she will no doubt take up with me later, eh, Dear?"

"That's right, Nelson. Just look on your desk where the 'Need' list is, and you will see a list of items that I suggested you order when I heard about this wedding," Maria answered archly. They all laughed at Maria's having bested Nelson at merchandising. They drove up to the Tift home, said goodnight to their friends, and went inside. Charles was waiting at the store and excused himself after chatting a while about who was there to attend the wedding. Soon he left them to go to his temporary quarters at the warehouse.

Nelson took Maria on a buggy trip around Albany and the nearby towns and villages. She was proud of her young husband and thought him very attractive with his five feet ten inches of military-straight bearing, broad shoulders, slim hips and waist, fair complexion, blue eyes, and blond hair. She had learned that he was quiet but firm and would step in and take command when he felt it necessary. She had found his manners and speech with her, at first, very stilted and sometimes that his conversation was reminiscent of old English novels, but she soon saw beneath this veneer the real, ambitious, eager young man who would jump impulsively into an undertaking and wonder about how he would do it later. He was given to worry and second guessing himself and would drive himself unmercifully to make whatever it was come to pass. She knew that her husband unconsciously used her as a sounding-board when his plans were being formulated and that her reactions were carefully analyzed by him.

They went from old Palmyra to Indian Springs where they drank the delightfully cold waters. They rested and waded in the beautiful springs a little and then went on to Starksville, which Maria had never been permitted to visit because of its notorious reputation. It was a very good business town, but its saloons were notorious and the homicide rate very high. Numerous armed marshals patrolled the territory, and Doctor Mercer was often called when someone had been shot and needed treatment. Starksville was not a port city but produced much cotton. The people tried sometimes to build cotton boxes and ship their harvest in the pitchtar waterproofed containers, shipping from nearby Danville around the shoals and rapids down to Albany to be loaded on the steamers or barges towed by the steamers.

They made the trip to Danville so that Nelson could talk to the men there. Those living around Danville said that Starksville was an old Indian town, as had been most of the little villages in the area. Nelson talked with and introduced Maria to Lott Warren. He and Warren talked about getting the river dredged and made more navigable; they discussed crops and the weather in general. Lott told Nelson that signs were encouraging for the stagecoach and the mail to run on the west side of the Flint before long. Maria was introduced to Mr. Glover who took another order for a cotton box. They crossed on Tinsley's ferry to Pindertown and talked with William J. Ford, who was ill, and with Hiram Vines, who would be next in line for the position of postmaster, if Ford had to give it up or if he passed away. They also talked much about the stage and made better arrangements for getting the people picked up across the river from the steamboat landing where the ferry crossed at Albany. They drove by Oakfield and talked with a visitor there who was from Cedar Springs down in Early County. Robert Winn Sheffield had much to say, and Nelson promised to see him on his next trip to Early County.

The buggy travelers were again in Albany a little after dusk. Maria was fascinated by the glorious day she had spent with her husband; and with the many things she had seen and the people she had met. They decided to go out to the old "Blue Hole" via the great round lime sink west of Albany and cut back through from Byron to Hartford Road, thence out to Gillionville to visit with their friends out that way next Sunday. Maria knew that some of the people from the older settlements around Albany considered them "Johnnie-come-latelys" and knew that her husband was doing a little ground-breaking here and there in addition to the historical and social aspects of their visits.

Nelson showed his wife the mysterious sand dunes across the Flint River. Many said these huge dunes were left by the great ocean that had formerly covered this part of the country. Nelson had a theory that the river had deposited the white sands for thousands of years on its eastern banks and that the winds had blown the sand over and deposited it in the impressive dunes, sand pits, and ridges. They drove out about four miles to Blue Springs, which was on the Alligator Stage road. Maria could hardly credit the sight her eyes beheld when she gazed down into the huge cavern where the cold water gushed upward, forming their own fairly large blue river of ice-cold water, and flowing on to the Flint River.

Time flew by for the young couple. They were selling land and merchandise at an accelerated pace, but they were not always getting good security. Real money was tight and most specie was shaky; nevertheless, they felt they were getting somewhere in the world. Certainly this town was growing by leaps and bounds. Summer passed into fall and on November 29, 1838, Charles, who had been on a visit to Key West, returned to Albany bringing brothers Julius and Lucius Tift with him. Never had Maria seen such a reunion between brothers. She knew that by the time Nelson remembered to return and introduce his wife to his brothers that her eyes were red from laughing and crying at their happiness and that she scarcely looked presentable.

Maria had been told that Lucius was a deaf mute and so forewarned, she made the introductions easier by merely embracing each as Nelson presented them to her. Julius looked very much like Nelson and Charles, but Maria thought Lucius to be a little heavier with perhaps darker hair. His fair skin and blue eyes were identical with the other Tifts. Maria had prepared dinner to celebrate the arrival of the visitors, after which Charles and Nelson had to take their brothers all over town and even into the outskirts of Albany. The visitors were shown everything that had been done, and was being planned for the future. They were introduced as "some more Tifts" to one and all.

A steamer came upstream and was going back to Appalachicola about four days after the brother arrived. Lucius took the steamer back to Apalachicola and would book passage on a packet from there to Key West. They saw him aboard, and Nelson had a few words in private with the steamer captain about Lucius' impediment. The Captain promised to watch out for him and to leave word with the master of the packet he would take to Key West.

Julius spent a month in Albany. Everyone in Albany loved this "other" Tift as they were wont to call him. Nelson and Maria tried to interest this "other" Tift in two or three young girls in the area so that he might be tempted to stay and cast his lot with them, but he finally told them, "I surely do hate to leave you and Albany. I am indeed fond of this place and the good folk here who have been so kind to me, but my heart is set on going on to Mobile to work with Hannah Carolyn and her husband at the Waverly House."

"Yes, but what can they possibly offer you there that we don't have here?" Maria asked.

"Ah, well, you'll laugh at me!" Alfred Noyes has a young sister, Kate Noyes, whom I just can't get out of my mind. That is why I cannot stay here with you wonderful people."

"Kate Noyes. Why she must be just a little girl! I can't believe this. You must be jesting?" Nelson said incredulously.

"Yes, a little girl about like me, I wager. Oh, Nelson, I think I have really known that there was a girl in his life.

I thought it must be in Key West or perhaps Mystic," Maria said, and added, "We want you here, but you had better go to Mobile before she finds another young man who is available."

"Oh, Maria, you don't think she really might do that, do you?"

"Julius, you have heard the old saw about a bird in hand being better than two in the bush," Maria answered darkly, but teasingly.

Nelson saw that the die was cast. Both he and Charles were now thoroughly amused at the way Maria was teasing their brother and said, "Boy, we had better get you on the first boat or stage going toward Mobile. We will certainly miss you, and we want you to come back any time you can. We do not, however, want to be blamed if you stay with us now and later accuse us for your being an old grumpy bachelor the rest of your life." They talked nearly all night about their childhood home in Mystic, their brothers and sisters, and Mother Hannah. Nelson asked about Robert and old String Bean and other friends in Connecticut. They talked over the unfortunate domestic situation between Amos Chapman and his family and agreed that it would be better if Amos left Key West for good instead of traveling back and forth the way he had for some time.

After the departure of their guest, Nelson and Charles settled down into the routine of running the town. The big mill was working "can to can't" since Nelson had become a partner with Alexander Shotwell in the cedar lumber business. They were cutting and floating the logs into the big mill where Uncle Billy and Brother Mercer further processed them for market. Huge rafts of logs were floated and towed down to Apalachicola to be loaded on barges there for transport to market in New York City. Maria was looking over the books one evening and asked the question, "Nelson, do you know whether Alfred Noyes was to give Julius one thousand a year and found or if Julius has to furnish his own provender and lodging?"

"Wait a minute. I am not sure at all; I don't think it ever came up. But then I am certain that it must be 'with found', as he could not possibly pay his own on that kind of salary, even if he were here and living out in 'sand town', 'sandy bottom', or 'Smokey Row'," Nelson answered.

"Not to change the subject, but do you think we should continue to accept cotton for goods and services?"

"Dear, if we do not, the owners of the cotton will have to go elsewhere. You know there are already three firms in the cotton buying and mercantile business, just as we are, right here in Albany," Nelson answered.

"Well, the reason I asked is that we will pretty soon be forced to eat cotton and land lots if we continue to accept bales of cotton and titles to land we may or may not ever even see," Maria said with a shrug of her shoulders.

"I know, my dear, but the way I look at it is that if these folks did not believe in me and count on me in emergencies, they would not have come here to our town in the first place. As long as I am financially able, I shall help them to help themselves," Nelson said softly but with firm resolution.

"Of course, you are right, my husband. You make me, a minister's daughter, ashamed of myself, for you have more of the milk of human kindness and compassion in your little finger than most of us have in our entire bodies." She sighed a wistful little sigh and added, "I just love and admire you with all my heart and soul."

"Now Maria, my dear, let's not become overwhelmed with my goodness lest we do end up, as you say, 'eating cotton and land lots'," Nelson laughed teasingly.

"Can't we do something about these drifters, ne'er-do-wells, drunks, and bullies who are slowly converging on Sandy Bottom? Some of the ladies told me just today that they were afraid to come to our store. They were afraid of being accosted by these dabauchers and thieves."

"I know it is bad, Maria. I did everything in my power to get a charter of incorporation from the State Legislature. All of the good citizens here are helping me. We can now see much progress in that direction. When we get that charter, we will have the authority to have a mayor, a council, and the legal tools to deal with the hard cases in Albany. We will rid ourselves of these undesirables. Just today, I had to cane a man out of town, not because he was drunk, as some of our citizens get into that deplorable condition now and again, but because this man stays in that condition and is a constant menace to the town and its population, especially the citizens and storekeepers of Sandy Bottom," Nelson said with deep feeling.

"When you filed your petition for your charter, did you stress the need for law and order here?"

"Oh, yes! We told the Legislature that we would be able to control the confidence men, drunks, bullies, gamblers, and ne'er-do-wells only if they would grant us the charter," Nelson answered emphatically. He then added with tenderness and concern, "But, Maria, now that you are with child, I wish you would stop worrying about these things and let me worry about them. When are we expecting the baby?"

"I was talking with Mrs. John Mock the other day, and she agrees with me that the baby won't come before September."

A. C. Sellers and old Ben left Albany with two wagon loads of lumber cut to the specifications given by Mr. William McAllister of Franklyn, Alabama, for the barouche he was to build for Nelson. There were also some supplies on the wagons for crossroad stores between Albany and Fort Gaines. Sellers would drive the lead wagon with Ben behind him in a two-horse covered wagon. The weather was ideal, and the Hartford Trail was in good shape for such a trip.

On the twenty-fifth of May, 1838, Shotwell and Tift sold nearly their entire stock of goods at an auction. Nelson went to Hawkinsville by stage the next day, where he received his script for the Flint River Land Company and went on to Macon to make the necessary arrangements to exchange some of the script for a thousand acres of land in the first district of Baker County, known as the Goodwin Place. He then settled the note and account with H. B. King for eight hundred fifty dollars, with a sight draft from LaFitte to the cashier at the Bank of Charleston, South Carolina, for collection by Daniel Lawhorn.

Nelson went to the state capital at Milledgeville where he mingled with the county representatives with whom he talked politics a little and reasoned a lot until he was assured that there would be a charter for the town of Albany in Baker County. One of the men he talked to was from Connecticut, but now was in business in Clinton, Georgia. Samuel Criswold had an iron foundry in Clinton. He manufactured cotton gins, grist mills, printing presses and other machinery of iron. Sam asked Nelson if he were part of the Tift family from over at

Blountsville, Georgia. Nelson told him they were cousins from Groton, Connecticut, and they corresponded from time to time. Nelson told Sam that he might be interested in doing business with him in the future, and Sam assured him that it would be a pleasure to serve him.

On the fifth of June, 1838, the return trip to Albany was made by stagecoach. Maria was delighted to have Nelson back home. Charles was on the Kinchafoonee Creek getting out more cedar. He had three hands along and Maria reported that a young man named Tinsley was there with him. Nelson made a mental note of this, as A. C. Sellers and Charlie Tison had mentioned that there was a good young man named Charlie Tinsley who wanted to go with the floating mill and follow the cedar cutting. This could be downright confusing as he had it in his mind that Charlie Tison had worked for Tinsley at the ferry, and now Charlie Tinsley would be working for Charlie Tison cutting cedars on the Kinchafoonee. Come to think of it, with Charles Tift up there, it was really confusing, as that made three men by the name of Charles in one little work crew, Nelson paused, shook his head, and determined to ask A. C. Sellers what that "C" in his name stood for.

There was also a letter from Rawls and King, one from Mobile, one from Key West, and one from the bank at Columbus. Nelson picked up the one from Rawls and King, broke open the seal, and opened it. He read the letter over twice, then turned and told Maria, "The old boys are headed here for a final settlement with me, but I am ready for them. Now I must go and get some of this trail dust off my clothes and take a bath. I hope you are not too put out with me for bringing back all my clothing dirty." Maria stood speechless as her husband dumped the dirtiest and most crumpled assortment of wearing apparel on the floor that she had ever seen. But one thing that fell from the "war bag" caught and held Maria's attention. There among her husband's toilet articles and dirty clothes was an immaculate, beautifully wrapped gift.

"Oh, you didn't forget me," squealed Maria like a little girl. She was not so excited that she did not take her time unwrapping the present carefully in order to save the hard to come by paper and the ribbons. A small, white, leatherbound Bible lay on top of a similar sized and shaped white leather case. Gingerly, Maria opened this "surprise" and exclaimed happily, "Oh, you must be the most thoughtful husband in the whole wide world. Who but you would think of such a contradiction of choices?" There inside the delicate little case was a complete selection of toilette articles, everything Maria had ever seen or heard about to assist a lady who wanted to look her best with a minimum of effort.

"Ah, Nelson, I wager I am the only woman in Baker County with one of these genuine French Toilette sets. It is so beautifully and tastefully bound! Why, I thought at first glance that you had brought two identical white leatherbound Bibles."

Rawls and King came to Albany for the showdown with Nelson Tift. Everybody who was living in Baker County knew who they were as soon as they set foot in town. Several malcontents who nefarious activities had been curbed by Nelson were heard to remark, "Let's see our Connecticut Yankee get out of this fine kettle of fish he has spawned." The vast majority of Albany people felt that the town's founder would rise to the occasion as he always had up to this point. They proved to be right in this assumption when Messers. Rawls and King left Albany fully paid up and having relinquished any and all of their claims on the town of Albany and Nelson Tift.

It seemed that John Rawls had secretly coveted a small lot in Hawkinsville that happened to be quite near his bank. Nelson had quietly acquired this key piece of property through his friends in Macon. Both Rawls and King wanted one large, cultivated plantation in southwest Georgia. Nelson knew of this desire and was ready with the solution. With one stroke of the pen, the Rawls and King claims of Albany and its founder were settled when Nelson Tift offered the lot in Hawkinsville and the huge Goodwin Place Plantation. The transaction was completed and both parties completely satisfied. They parted as friends. Nelson knew that if he had traded with a southwest Georgia businessman he would not have received more than four thousand dollars for the Goodwin Place.

Forewarned had been forearmed in this instance, and as John Rawls told his partner on the stage going back to Hawkinsville, "Just as I told you, I have always felt that boy would do the right thing. Here you were a year ago saying that Nelson had ruined us with his big plans."

"John, don't you remember all the things you said about Nelson Tift after we had almost given up on Albany as a trading town and certainly as head of navigation on the Flint River? You remember what you said when he obligated us for that steamboat full of merchandise to be sold to no one and nothing but a wilderness of pines occupied by a handful of penniless sodbusters?"

"Oh, granted that I might have lost my temper a little; but later I did tell you that I thought he would make restitution, didn't I?" John asked in a hurt tone.

"You sure did, John, especially after you had him in position to put him in jail if he could not produce some nearly impossible payments with a mighty short time." King laughed and slapped his partner on the shoulder making the trail dust fill the close quarters inside the swaying stage.

"Well, all's well that ends well! I will remind you there are still a few loose ends, minor though they may be, hanging fire at the county seat at Newton," John told his partner with a sly wink.

"No, I thought this pretty well closed us out with the Tift boy. John, you never turn loose, do you?" King said with wonder in his voice.

"Business, my boy," said John Rawls, then asked, "and how do you think a businessman like me got in a position to handle the business I do?"

Several of Nelson's friends came to see him. They wanted to discuss politics, urging him to take a more active interest in the running of Baker County and the new town of Albany. Nelson did not tell them, but there were a number of problems he was wrestling with outside the scope of local politics. The Lawhorn draft was not accepted. Old Pierre had passed away while in New Orleans, and thirty-seven bales of cotton would not cover the amount. He did get an order on the cotton for the proceeds and paid the Atkinson note to Montgomery for black hire, thus closing out the Tift-Atkinson debts. Charles informed him that the cedar was ready to be shipped down to Apalachicola and from there by barge to New York City. Nelson knew that it would be impossible for him, at this time, to make the trip. He informed Charles that he would have to take the responsibility once they got the logs to Apalachicola.

A meeting was called to appoint men and women on the various committees to form and expedite plans for the Fourth of July celebration. For one solid week, every home, business, and business house in the northern part of Baker County was full of plans, talk, and work toward THE BIG DAY. When it came, the barbecue was bigger, the dance was bigger and better, the speeches were shorter but better, and the crowd was bigger and louder — and hungrier than ever before.

Word came from Newton that Rawls had sued on a note for one thousand two hundred fifty dollars. The note was on H. Atkinson and endorsed by M. Chastain. There was a big question in Nelson's mind as to which party was really liable, and he told Maria and Charles, "It seems to me that Chastain will be bound for the note, but I will go to Newton tomorrow and see about it." Nelson was in Newton the next day when he heard the rumor that Atkinson had left for Texas. The authorities at the courthouse said they would agree to hold off taking any kind of action until the muddled state of affairs surrounding the note was cleared somewhat which might be at the next term of court.

Nelson told Maria that he had a chance to get rid of some paper he was holding by getting three blacks for two thousand three hundred fifty dollars and a two-horse barouche that he could get for six hundred in notes due him.

"We will be able to see that the blacks get better treatment here with us than they are getting wherever they are now and goodness knows there is plenty of work for one and all. I know the barouche can be utilized to great advantage as the rest of us around here need some sort of transportation when you are away. I want your word that no family until is being broken up in order for these blacks to be brought here. I cannot make them happy with us if they are snatched up from their loved ones and sent here broken-hearted. I think you are right in getting rid of some of this paper wealth. It seems lately that every person I meet on the street owes us or we owe him," complained Maria as she agreed to the proposed changes.

"Well put, and very true, my dear. I perceive that the good professors in LaGrange taught you girls a little about the realities of life as well as how to serve and sip tea — and look pretty," Nelson laughingly teased his wife.

"You know, my husband, if some of those girls could see the tasks that I perform here from daylight until after dark, they simply would not believe their eyes. They thought me a little simpering, helpless, 'Miss goody-goody' preacher's daughter. I had to appear so to be there." Maria sighed and added, "Go on and get out of here, and let me get your things ready for that foolish trip down the river with the cedar rafts tomorrow."

The August sun beat down unmercifully on the men who were guiding the big cigar-shaped cedar rafts down the Flint. They had forced the passage of the rafts through whirlpools, suck holes, over and around shoals, and found it much easier than the comparable task of bringing a barge or steamer through the same spots at this time of the year. They tied up below Bainbridge and prepared to spend the night. Nelson was going back to Albany in the morning by stage. Charles would take the cedar by barges on to New York City. The mosquitoes were a constant menace to the men. Nelson ordered everyone ashore where they cleared a big circle and built a campfire. Each man had a piece of cheesecloth that he pulled over his head and let fall down over his shoulders; this kept most of these winged demons of the devil out of the men's eyes, nostrils, and mouths so that they could get a little rest before another hard day of getting the rafts down the river. They slept intermittently, rolled up in their bed rolls, on the ground in the clearing.

At first light there was a loud yell, "Bear in camp!" The fire had burned down to a pile of reddish-grey ashes, and a big black bear had moved into the circle looking for a meal. The big bear was as alarmed as the men who were jumping out of their bed rolls and bumping into each other in their efforts to get away from the bear who was himself trying to escape from all the commotion. There was much good-natured laughing and joshing afterwards over the incident as the men started going back onto the rafts to get some breakfast and making arrangements for casting off for another day on the river. They knew that with the sun and the heat would come the hoards of black gnats, flies, mosquitoes, and bees. All the men dreaded getting black gnats in their nostrils and their eyes, and every man-jack of them knew that he would have to go through discomfort and misery that day with these annoying insects. The first men on the raft each morning had to run the 'gators off into the water. The big amphibians climbed up on the rafts during the night looking for a meal of watersnakes who had made the rafts their temporary homes. Most of the snakes left the rafts once the men came aboard to start moving around with the long keelboat type poles that they used to guide the rafts' progress down to the Bay. Every now and then a water moccasin or a big timber rattler would attempt to stake his claim on some part of the raft, even in broad day light, and the men would have to beat him off with their poles or throw him overboard where a 'gator would invariably surface and grab the snake in his great jaws.

Nelson returned to Albany by the Alligator Stage line, and Ben brought him across the Flint on the ferry. Maria filled a tub with hot, soapy water and her husband took a well-deserved (and much needed) bath. After bathing and changing clothes, he told Annie Maria about the trip and about how well it had gone up to this point. Maria was amused by the story of the bear getting into camp and had a dozen questions about how they lived, worked, and got their meals while on the river.

On August 17, 1838, Shotwell and Tift agreed that each would shoulder his part of the existing debts of their company, and to settle them.

"Nelson, I will take care of the New York debt, which amounts to one thousand eight hundred dollars, and the five hundred in steamboat stock." Alexander paused a moment and added, "Here, let me see if that is right. Hand me the ledger."

"Yes, I think that is about right, Alexander," Nelson replied as he handed the ledger over to Shotwell. "That will leave me to take care of Cobb and Company, A. B. Duncan and Company, Arnett, Ellison, Rope and Day, Mr. Cowart, Bond and Sheffield." Nelson paused and then asked, "Is that about the way you have it, Alexander? How do you want to divide our holdings left from the partnership? It is strictly up to you!"

"Nelson, Maria was telling me that you are holding more notes and mortgages than you should be and that it became embarrassing to both of you at times. I don't live here and would not be bothered that way. This is your home, and you can watch over and tend to the real estate, so why don't we made an estimate of notes and mortgages due as compared to our joint real estate holdings and, if compatible, you take the real property and I the paper?"

Shotwell sat back as both worked quietly for ten or fifteen minutes, pausing to slap at insects or wipe sweat from their hands and faces now and then. Shotwell's chair made a scratching sound as he pushed back from the table, leaned back on the back two legs of his cane-bottomed chair and said, "How say ye, Scribe?"

Nelson looked up at his friend, smiled his warmest smile and said, "I believe you are right when you weigh the good and bad, the pros and the cons of both, as they do come up fairly even. As you say, I can do more with less personal involvement and embarrassment, if I deal in the land rather than with the notes." The two friends shook hands and signed the necessary papers and that was it. Nelson now owned all the property formerly held by their company, and Shotwell owned the bills due them and other paper assets of their partnership.

"Do you think I should pack a lunch and a container of water for our ride up to Lee County?" Maria asked Nelson one bright autumn day. She had been wanting to take another long ride in the barouche and to visit with friends and relations.

"It might be advisable, Maria. I do not anticipate any touble, but you know how a wheel can come loose, a spoke fall out or there could be a complete breakdown with the wheel coming off, and everything else. We can stop for a picnic along the road," Nelson said.

The buggy ride was taken in perfect weather. It was September, and the weather was beautiful. Even some of the gnats seemed to have departed as there was just a suggestion of fall in the air. The team of black horses clickety-clicked sharply down the road and to the edge of Albany and over Kinchafoonee Creek. Nelson wore a lightweight, long duster and his best dress hat. Maria also wore a little duster with a light shawl tied over her wide-brimmed hat and under her chin. The trappings of the horses and the newly waxed and shining little barouche made quite a smart looking rig as they sped along. Ben considered it a personal insult to him if any of the equipment in his charge was seen in public when it was not "up to snuff."

Maria remarked that there seemed to be far too many watermelons in the field that had not been gathered. Her husband agreed with her, but added that he thought it was "turn-out time" for the livestock and that this particular melon field might have been left for the animals. They visited with the Jordans, the Mercers, and the J. Davis families. Mr. Davis insisted on swapping horses with them for the return trip. This was a regular custom when visiting with folks, and the horses would be exchanged at the next opportunity. It was a lovely day, and the young couple thoroughly enjoyed the day, although they were worn out by the time they drove up to their place in Albany just as the sky was reddening with sunset in the west.

Brother Mercer brought Nelson a letter from Charles. They had gotten the cedar to Apalachicola and had it ready to ship to New York City, where it would be measured and paid for at ten cents a foot. All hands, except the three that Charles had kept to help him get the cedar loaded on the barges, were available for trips upstream and just waiting for capable keelboat men to take them up.

On the twenty-second of September, 1838, Nelson drove the new barouche down the sandy road to Newton. The Atkinson note suit was thrown out of court, as the Judge found out that Chastian had already paid it; however, John Gillian told Nelson that Royal and Company were going to enter suit against him for some old notes that had come back to haunt him. "I know how you must feel, Nelson. These things just simply would not happen if the state would go on and give Albany its charter so you-all could exercise some sort of control over things like this without having to be notified and make a trip down here to squelch one nuisance only to find that another had emerged while you were on the way back home." The unhappy Nelson made the long drive back to Albany feeling, as he told Maria that night, "All broken down."

The new building was almost completed so Nelson sold the warehouse and the house to James Bond. He and Maria set up housekeeping in the nearly-completed building, Maria doing her own housework and sewing. The New York paper carried an item in the shipping news regarding the Brig

'Waukulla' arriving with cedar from Albany, Georgia. Mr. Stittman brought Nelson the paper and said he was getting ready to leave by stage from New York City when he saw the item in the paper. Mr. Stittman also said that he had seen and talked to Charles. Maria commented that it was highly unlikely that Charles had not written and that she believed Mr. Stittman had beaten the letter home. Nelson did some ledger work and decided to send four hundred dollars to Macon and to send two hundred in payment toward the four hundred outstanding at Key West. He settled all wages owed except to Charles, settled the Arnett bill to S. C. Stephens, and rented out a small store for four hundred dollars a year.

The sad news came that William Ford had passed away in Pindertown. Nelson and some of his friends attended the funeral and met with Mr. Hiram W. Vines who was in line for the appointment as postmaster. Nelson noted that Mr. Ford was buried near another friend, Mr. J. Jackson. Charlie Tison was also at the services and told Nelson that his father was failing badly in health and the end seemed near for the old-timer. Charlie rode back to the ferry where they heard the bad news. The elder Tison had indeed passed away while they were attending Mr. Ford's services. Nelson told the others to go back to Albany without him as he wanted to be with Charlie and his father for the rest of the afternoon.

"Tell Maria what has happened and that I will get a horse and come on in after the funeral tomorrow," Nelson told his friend, John Jackson.

Congressman Lott Warren was doing everything in his power in Washington to get the stage coach to run west of the Flint River. There were now over five thousand people in Lee County; two thousand three hundred whites and two thousand seven hundred blacks.

Things had just not worked out for the Bond boys at the warehouse and store, and Nelson bought both back from them for less than five thousand dollars. Colonel Robert Bereridge was then given an option on the property. Nelson entered into a large transaction to acquire a great parcel of land in Baker and Early Counties across the Chickasawhatchee Creek. Charles was afraid that this huge parcel of land could become a burden on his brother, but Nelson assured him that when he saw the land, he would understand the transaction. Then came the shocking news that Colonel Bereridge had passed away in St. Joseph. Of course, this cancelled out any chance of a deal for the property at the corner of Broad and Front Streets.

On the twenty-seventh of December, 1838, was enacted the long-awaited charter incorporating the town of Albany, in Baker County, on lots 323, 324, 333, 334, of the first district thereof. Section five of the act said "and be it further enacted that the said Tomlinson Fort, Nelson Tift, and J. C. Harris and their associates be and they are hereby declared a body corporate with power to make all by-laws, rules, and regulations of their government which they may deem proper, etc." The document further stated that "and be it further enacted that Tomlinson Fort, Nelson Tift, and Jeptha C. Harris and their associates have the privilege of building and constructing a bridge over the Flint River at or near the town of Albany on their own land at any point above or below the said town with the power to establish tolls as follows: from three cents an animal, six cents, twenty-five cents, thirty-seven and a half cents, fifty cents and up to seventy-five cents for the largest multi-animal-drawn vehicles."

The lots on which Albany was being built had originally been "drawn" by James Harrison, Orren Wiggins, William Lindsey, and Littleberry Clanton, with each lot containing two hundred two and a half acres. Thus the town of Albany consisted of eight hundred and ten acres bounded on the north by Society Avenue, on the east by the Flint River, on the south by old Plantation Boundary Road, and on the west by Corporation Alley.

At a meeting called by some of his friends, Nelson was persuaded to make himself available as the Justice of the Inferior Court of Baker County and was duly elected. He later told these same friends, "There is little honor and some expenses involved here, both campaigning and in the performance of the duties of the office, but we all must do our part to insure law and order so that the county and the town can grow and be prosperous and the people happy."

Charles and Maria knew that Nelson had not spared himself or his horses in the extensive campaign he had waged all over Baker County in order to shake hands and talk to every possible voter in every precinct. Nelson made many lifelong friends during this simple election for a humble office.

The old families of Baker County, who were pioneers long before Nelson came to southwest Georgia, were beginning to recognize and to respect the young transplant from Connecticut and now were showing this high regard for him at the polls on election day. On the twenty-first of May, 1839, Nelson attended a committee session at the State Capitol at Milledgeville as the Representative from Baker County, and was impressed by the eloquence of some of the distinguished delegates. Judge Winn from Chatham County presided at the meeting. Pay to the delegates was only five dollars a day. Nelson rode up to the Capitol with J. C. Harris and paid his own expenses, which amounted to fifty dollars. Governor Charles James McDonald was introduced to Nelson and some of his friends at a small reception, and the Governor asked some very intelligent questions about Albany in Baker County. It was apparent that Governor McDonald did not care too much for President Martin Van Buren but thought that he would "do what he considered was best for his country."

As Maria's time to give birth came closer and closer, the soon-to-be father felt honor-bound to stay closer and closer to his wife and the house. This was the last thing in the world that Maria wanted, and she went to great lengths to discourage him from forever being underfoot around the house and to persuade him to go about his business in his usual manner. On September sixth, 1839, Maria gave birth to a fine little girl. Dr. Gilbert was with her. Mrs. Mock, Mrs. Jackson, Mrs. Harris, and Mrs. Mercer supported the doctor and all went well. Never had news passed so quickly. Soon the whole countryside knew that the first white child had been born in Albany. Nelson felt confused and inadequate and could never really remember his actions during that day. The baby was given the name Annie Elizabeth Tift, and Nelson tried to compose himself long enough to write to Mother Hannah, Grandfather Solomon, the boys at Key West, and his sister and Alfred Noyes at Mobile. Two days later, he also wrote to selected friends in Augusta, Charleston, and Hawkinsville and asked them to pass the word about his new daughter to his friends in their areas.

One week after the child was born, Charles came to Nelson with a cane fishing pole and some bait and told him that Maria had asked him to send her husband off to the river to fish as she could get nothing done around the house or with the new baby with the fathers always underfoot. Nelson went fishing with John Jackson, James Bond, and old Doc Meals. They caught a forty-pound sturgeon, a nice catch of bream, and several sizeable bass.

"Now you can get back to town and your business and let Maria run the house and take care of that fine little girl, Nelson," laughed John Jackson.

The summer of 1839 proved profitable to the Tift brothers and on the ninth of December, 1839, Charles Tift sat down with his brother while they entered new business into their ledger concerning some local transactions. Nelson had a pile of deeds and notes in front of him, and Charles was at the desk, the ledger before him, with pen and quill in hand.

"Put down lots two ninety-eight, two ninety-nine in the first district of Baker County, lot two eighty-two in second district and lot two sixty-seven in third district. Now about this lot two hundred ninety-seven in the first district that I sent John Boggs down to Monticello, Florida, to purchase. Well, we might as well go on and put it down, too. We sold town lots thirty-four and thirty-six on Pine Street for five hundred sixty dollars, and I sold Solomon Mitchell an acre lot on Pine. That's lot number seventy-three, for one hundred dollars. Now don't put this one down, as I gave the gentlemen his money back and invited him to leave town before sundown. Of course, you know that I refer to Mr. Ming of Hawkinsville who had the effrontery and gall to show up here with his houseful of ladies of the evening. All right now: John W. Houghton and John Hatfield have taken care of the New York debt, and we are at last free of that one."

"Nelson, how about this Spalding Railroad thing that is being offered for pledges around Albany? What do you think about it?"

"Charles, they want us to subscribe five hundred thousand, and I think we will get about two hundred and fifty thousand. I have personally subscribed for two thousand five hundred, but I want you to let your conscience be your guide. I will say this: I cannot refuse the very people who would bring in the much-needed railroad; however, I am not recommending that you strip yourself and perhaps lose everything," Nelson replied.

The 1840 Fourth of July celebration went off well, except for the fights between the drunks and the poor harried politicians that were shouted down by the drunken men every time they tried to make a speech. Some of the people who were tired of the political speeches were secretly delighted to have parts of the talks interrupted and were silently hoping for the drunks to win some of the innumerable fist fights which broke out. At last, a semblance of order was restored, the cannon fired, and the barbecue and other foods laid out on the tables especially built for the occasion. Cakes, pies, chicken, and quail made these tables groan under their weight. The invocation was given, the colors hoisted, and everybody ate heartily of the delicious food.

There was street dancing when the area had been cleared. Ater the dancing, the people went inside to hear the Reverend Shackleford read the Declaration of Independence. J. C. Harris gave a stirring oration followed by a benediction by Nelson Tift, after which a torchlight procession followed. During the evening, an appeal was made for funds for the railroad that was being organized by General Bisbane, who had acquired his rank in the Seminole Indian Wars.

Bad feelings had been building up between John S. Marlin and Nelson Tift for many months. Neither man really wanted trouble, but at last the day arrived when trouble could no longer be averted. Nelson had bought Marlin out, lock, stock and barrel, and had paid him off with land on the Kinchafoonee Creek. Unbiased appraisers said that the value of the land that Marlin had received was much greater than the four thousand four hundred sixty-one dollars that Marlin had been due, but Marlin continued to say he had been swindled by Nelson Tift. This claim was what ultimately triggered the confrontation between the two. Never had two more unlikely gladiators met in full public view and neither participant was ever able to explain to himself or to his friends exactly how it happened; nevertheless, a knock down-drag out fist fight erupted between the two at the corner of Jackson and Pine

Streets. Marlin pulled a dirk, but a friend of Nelson Tift, a Mr. Gibson, saw the dirk and handed his friend a sturdy pole with which Nelson beat Marlin until "he was sensible."

Mr. Gibson later told his many listeners, "Nelson saw that the man was beaten and stepped back from him. Marlin got up slowly and approached his recent antagonist saying, 'Nelson, I have wronged you; I have no right to speak evil of you when you acted in good faith. I am not or have never been this kind of man, but it is the evil of drink, the approach of middle age, and the curse of gambling that has brought me to this low state. Now with your indulgence, not for me, but for the sake of my family, I beg you to forgive and forget and let me retire with my loved ones on the place on the Kinchafoonee that I have heard to be a veritable paradise.' " Of course, every listener wanted to know what Nelson's answer had been, and of course, Mr. Gibson gave his version of what his friend Nelson Tift had said, "Ah, my friend, it is I who should be begging your forgiveness and that of the good people of Albany who have witnessed a sad thing between two responsible, God-fearing citizens. Here, let me help you back to the store where Mrs. Tift will be happy to assist you in cleaning up so that you and I can walk down the streets of Albany again as friends."

At the end of the year, 1840, the news came of the birth of a son, Henry Harding Tift, to Phoebe Harding Tift, the second wife of Amos Chapman. The seven-year-old Lewis Samuel Tift would stay with his mother in the Bahamas at Green Turtle Key. Nelson had often discussed this domestic relations problem in his family with Maria, and they agreed that Amos had nothing to be ashamed of and thought he did right to start another family under the circumstances. Of course, they both knew that they would have to let Charles go to Key West when Amos returned to Mystic, but they had known for a long time that it was coming. Parting would be a gentle sorrow.

"Nelson, what did cause them to drift apart?" Maria asked.

"Dear, I believe that there was a deep difference of opinion between them on everything from religion to social position. As you know, Amos is a quiet man with deep personal convictions and feelings which he is reluctant to discuss, while young Sam's mother is very witty, outgoing and quite society-minded, and here the two just never could agree." Nelson said this with a sad shake of his head before adding, "Well, I guess I had better go over and talk with Charles about all this."

Chapter 9

On the fifteenth of September, 1840, Nelson wrote a rebuttal to a piece that had appeared in the *Columbus Enquirer* saying that Albany had a bad climate and was very unhealthful. John Jackson had brought the Columbus paper to Nelson and said, "Nelson, irresponsible reporting such as this can sound the death knell of Albany or any other young town and ruin people such as you and I who have everything we own tied up in building the town. I think that you are most qualified to send an answer to this item, and I believe you to be well enough known in southwest Georgia for people to pay attention to what you write."

Men listened when John Jackson spoke, and Nelson was no exception to the rule. He had liked Jackson from the very first day they had met, and he had never changed that first impression. He had told Annie Maria several times that the coming of this man to Albany was the best piece of luck that had befallen the little town up to that point. One evening they had been talking before the open fire, and Nelson had said, "Maria, John Jackson was born in 1806 near the Virginia-Pennsylvania line. He fought with General Brisbane in the Seminole War in Florida in 1835 and was given a great tract of land near the beautiful St. Johns River for his services. John left South Carolina and came down here two years ago. Everyone in this district, whether in farming, cotton trading, or shipping, timber or mercantile, will tell you that John's word is his bond. I know that if Charles and I can't do business with a man, we try to steer him to John Jackson because we know he will be dealt with fairly and may come back to deal with us the next time for having guided him right in the first instance. I am certain that it was John who got General Brisbane interested in trying to form the railroad company and get a railroad here in Albany, and I do know that John has very strong influence in high places within our government."

"Oh, yes," Maria said as she shifted little Annie Elizabeth in her crib. "I have been told of that heartbreaking scene between John and his kinsman, Andrew Jackson, when the President took John out to Rachel's grave and told him how his enemies have slandered the President's beloved wife and caused her to grieve herself to death. They say that it nearly broke John's heart to see the old General come to pieces before his very eyes."

"Who told you about John and General Jackson?"

"Why, a very good friend of — ours, that's who. Don't you think I ever hear anything except that which originates in this room?"

"Now, now! I was not disputing your story, which, by the way, is true. I hear that John was told by his kinsman that this would be a good place for him to come and settle. There is much more to the story that I will tell you some day about an Indian chief's son that John is to look out for on the Kinchafoonee Creek," Nelson answered, fully aware that Maria loved a mystery and would hound him and give him no peace until he told her of the mysterious son of old Chief Menewa.

The Flint River was low, but the ninety-feet-by-fifteen-feet barge that belonged to John Jackson left for Apalachicola with one hundred bales of cotton aboard. The bales averaged four hundred fifty pounds each. Captain C. H. Blair was in command. Nelson believed that if this shipment made it to the Bay at this time of the year with the water level so low, much of the credit would have to go to the excellent work being done on the river by Captain James Glover, superintendent of river work.

Nelson and Maria urged Charles to attend a meeting of the Baptists that was being held to discuss the possibility of building an academy of learning in Albany. One prior meeting had been held, which had been attended by Nelson, Maria, and some of their friends as well as by many Baptists. The Reverend Jonathan Davis delivered an address at this particular meeting, and Charles thought that this minister was most persuasive in his reasoning as to the need for an academy. More than a thousand dollars were pledged at this meeting and work was begun on the building. Progress was slow on the new building, but eventually it was time for the dedication ceremonies and the grand opening of Albany's first center of learning.

Nelson wrote letters to Julius and Amos Tift and a letter of introduction for Wyle Lane to his brothers in Key West. Maria had been worried about the severe headaches her husband had been experiencing and urged him to cut down on his correspondence and the use of his eyes especially when he was forced to work by candle and lamplight. Maria had exhausted her collection of "potions" for the headaches and had a talk with Dr. Hillsman about her husband's symptoms when she visited her parents at Palmyra. Doctor Gilbert had prescribed some medication for Nelson but said he thought the real trouble was too much reading of law books by the fireplace.

The big cotton barge had made it to Apalachicola, and now Nelson felt it was time to get the "Edwin Forest" ready to make the run to the Bay. On the return trip, the boat could steam up to Forest Gaines and Columbus and then drop back down the Chattahoochee and into the Flint for Bainbridge and Albany. The run was made to Apalachicola without mishap. Nelson found things very dull and went on to Port St. Joseph to pick up some freight, most of which was steam mills and parts for mills that he had sold in southwest Georgia. He took another sea bath which he enjoyed very much. Upon return to Apalachicola he found that the authorities and the hotel people had been unable to shed any light on his missing wallet and money, and it occurred to him that perhaps it was because the guilt was embarrassing to them. The upriver run was a smooth one. Nelson and crew members visited with family and friends in Fort Gaines. William McAllister was in the midst of moving his family from Shorterville and Franklin, Alabama, across the river to Fort Gaines where he had purchased a big home from W. Ford on the same side of the street with the Dill House and the Brown home. Nelson was delighted to learn that his new barouche was ready to be taken aboard the steamer for shipment to Albany. He took dinner at the Dill House, and by the time he got back to the landing, the freight for Fort Gaines had been off-loaded and the cargo bound for Columbus was loaded.

Nelson went up to the Tavern on the bluff at Irwinton and found that half the citizens there were calling the town Eufaula, must as they had when he and Captain Watts had met Maria and her father there. Nelson met General William Wellborn, his cousin, Dr. Levi Thomas Wellborn, and the General's wife, the former Roxana Bethune, the daughter of the Georgia Surveyor General who had laid out the town of Columbus, Georgia. The General had been left with a weakened constitution by wounds received at the last Indian Battle of Alabama, the battle of Hobdy Bridge Campaign. The General had purchased the old Irwinton *Herald* but had sold it because of the lack of experienced help. The doctor had been persuaded by his cousin to come to the new town to practice medicine. The Wellborns invited Nelson to ride with them in their carriage to their new home on Livingston Street. Nelson found the house had two-story heavy columns, Doric capitals across the front, and a cantilevered balcony on the second floor. Both floors had identical plans, with wide center halls and two rooms on either side. Plaster on brick formed the great, heavy round columns across the front of the house. Roxana served tea and other refreshments. Several friends came in and were introduced to their guest before he returned to the landing to resume his upriver run to Columbus. It had been a charming interlude and Nelson had extracted a promise from his host and hostess that they would visit with him in Albany.

At the bank of Columbus, an agreement was reached to receive notes for which Nelson could sell property on one, two, and three years' time in exchange for Shotwell and Tift notes for the "Edwin Forest" and three barges. Mr. Davis, cashier, and Mr. Fountain, bank director, made the proposition to Nelson, with the provision that Nelson sign over a power-of-attorney to the bank to make titles when the money was paid, and endorse the notes. The agreement was reached without further qualifications between the parties.

When Nelson arrived at the landing, he was introduced to a man who had been waiting to see him about taking four horses aboard and caring for them until they could be delivered to their owner in Albany. Mr. Edward Payne was a small man and a very sincere individual.

"I sure hope you can see your way to taking these horses for me, Mr. Tift. I hate to think of having to drive them all the way to Albany and then getting back here the best I can. Do you think you might be able to take them off my hands?" the little man asked hopefully.

Nelson noticed a smart looking vehicle across the cobblestone street from which a lady was waving a handkerchief. He excused himself to Mr. Payne and started across the street saying over his shoulder, "Bring the animals down in the morning, Mr. Payne; I think I have a plan."

When Nelson saw who was in the carriage, his heart leaped up into his throat. The beautiful young Octavia Walton had grown into the beautiful Madam LaVert. She motioned him into the cab, and they rode several blocks to the hotel where she was staying until the stage left for Talbotton where she was to visit relatives. They had lunch and dinner together. Nelson saw her off on the early morning stage and went back to the boat. He called A. C. Sellers over and after explaining what Mr. Payne wanted them to do with his animals, said, "Listen, A. C., do you think 'Red Buck' can handle the 'Edwin Forest' back into Albany without me aboard?"

"Nelson, if you want to go back by stage, we can make it back fine. 'Red Buck' has been taking cotton boxes and barges downriver for a long time, and you have seen him handle the 'Edwin Forest'. I can handle the men, the freight, the boilers, and all. We know the rivers and the landings and should have no real trouble as the water level is just right."

Nelson turned and motioned to a big Negro who had reddish, freckled skin and rust colored hair. "Red Buck, Mr. Sellers will be in command of the cargo and the men back to Albany. You, as of this moment, are in command of the 'Edwin Forest' until you tie up at lower Broad in Albany."

"Thank you, Captain Tift. Any further orders before we cast off?" the big man asked without batting an eye.

"Yes. Mr. Sellers, have the men off-load my new barouche, some provisions for Ben and myself, some blankets and anything else that you think we might need for a three-day ride to Albany through the country." Nelson went back over and down the gang plank to the docks and talked with Mr. Payne.

"Get the horses, their feed and tack down here right away. I am going to drive them through the country to Albany. You may go along if you desire. To whom are they to be delivered?"

"Oh, no Sir, Mr. Tift. Thank ye, but I ain't lost nothing down through them woods," Mr. Payne said hastily. "By the way, how much are you going to charge me to drive the animals down there?"

"Not one cent, my good fellow. I just want to accommodate you and at the same time give my new barouche a good trial run. I can see the country and meet the good people between here and Albany. Now who are the horses to be delivered to?"

Mr. Payne was delighted over this turn of events and said quickly, "Oh, this is a transaction between my superior and a Mr. John Jackson of Albany who saw these horses and just had to own them."

"Ah, John Jackson! Well, I shall be most happy to deliver the animals to him as he is a favorite friend of mine. Now, please hurry back with the horses. My men have the barouche ready to go, filled with provisions, and they are ready to depart from Columbus," Nelson urged the little man who left in a flurry of motion and was off up the hill to Wewoka, or Columbus, as it was now called. Old Ben continued to pack things he thought they might need during the overland trip, into the gleaming barouche. Mr. Payne came back with the beautiful horses and two of the crew members helped get them hitched up to the barouche, while Nelson signed the receipt for them and handed it to the grateful Mr. Payne.

Nelson and Ben passed several little creeks and then took a ferry over the Upatoi Creek. This creek was wide and shallow, and Nelson wondered why they needed a ferry, and then noted that the ferry was really a floating bridge like the one down at Pachitla that Jonathan Neal had built to fluctuate with the rise and fall of water. They headed southeast from the old Indian town of Cusseta (Kashita) and changed horses every ten miles or thereabouts. They camped the first evening on the banks of the small, clear creek called Hitchiti. Nelson knew that it had been near here that the battle of Hitchiti had been fought between the Georgia Militia under Colonel Watson and forty armed Creek Indians in 1836.

"Ben, there had been a report that five hundred Red Stick Creeks had crossed the Chattahoochee. Colonel Watson and fifty men were sent out to investigate the report. Back where we used that ferry is where they first sighted what they thought to be about forty Indians who took cover and disappeared into the deep woods. The Colonel and his men pursued them, and the battle started when they caught them about a mile from here. Two Georgia militiamen were killed, and two were severely wounded. The Indians slipped away with their casualties, if any, and went back across the river."

Ben continued his cooking over the open fire they had built. He thought over what his master had just told him, all the while busily looking from under his eyebrows, trying to penetrate the thick growth all around them. After a thoughtful interval, he finally asked, "Mr. Nelson, do you calculate they is any of them Indian watching us from them woods right now?"

"Well, maybe, but just out of curiosity. You know that the largest part of all the Creek Indians and all of the Red Sticks have been gone from this country for several years now."

"Yes, suh, and I shore is glad 'cause tired as I'm is, it would be hard to keep my eyes open all night and my feet ready in case they was needed."

"Well, Indians or no Indians, you are going to sit right by that fire half the night and wake me up, and I will take over until daylight. Be sure the gun is loaded at all times. Under no circumstances are you even to think about taking a nap while you are on watch."

Except for the usual sounds of the deep woods during the night, nothing untoward happened, and they each got a little rest and were up bright and early. After a bite of breakfast, they hurriedly hitched up their team and continued toward the little frontier town of Lumpkin.

Nelson pulled up in front of a big two-story frame building that seemed to be Lumpkin's only inn. Bedingfield's was the stage stop between Blakely, Fort Gaines, and Columbus. It was situated on a corner of the square that was forming around the little temporary courthouse in the center. Doctor Byron Bedingfield had built the imposing hostelry, which was the meeting place and the social center of that part of the country.

While in Lumpkin, Nelson attended a poetry reading at the new two-story academy building which was attended by children of most of the prominent families in the area. Doctor Bedingfield had sent Ben down to some friends of his down at Barde's Grist Mill on Hodchodkee Creek to spend the night. After the poetry reading, some of the men returned to the Bedingfield Inn where Nelson sat and talked for hours with Mr. Thornton, Mr. Moye, Mr. Boynton, Mr. Sherwood, Doctor Bedingfield, who introduced him to many other local gentlemen: William Duncan, Needham R. Bryan, S. L. Lumpkin, Cullen Roberts, Mr. Evans, Mr. Sturdivant, Mr. Dennis, Mr. Mangham, Mr. Bridges, Reverend George Lynch Smith, whom he had also met at the academy. Reverend Smith told Nelson that he had held the first meeting of the Christian Church in Georgia near Lumpkin in 1837.

The stagecoach had deposited three men and a woman at the Inn. In order to avoid sleeping with his clothes on in a bed with several other similarly clad gentlemen of the road, Nelson got his bedroll from the barouche and slept on the floor on the parlor. After a hearty breakfast, Nelson went out to the stable to get the horses but found Ben already sitting in the barouche, the animals hitched up and ready to go, with the "swing" pair of horses tied to the back of the barouche. Seeing this, Nelson went back inside the inn and bade his host and hostess farewell, then followed the directions they gave him out of town and down across Hodchodkee (which he found meant "always muddy") Creek. They were traveling nearly due east now and passed through several villages. They stopped for crackers and cheese at a little settlement called "Hard Money."

They camped that night down the road about six miles in a grove of trees, near a bubbling spring that formed a little blue hole and ran off as a saucy little creek that disappeared into the green forest. They sat by the fire and talked. Ben told his master how his father had taught him to build a little water machine to grind up corn and other grains. He drew a picture in the sand. It was crude, but Nelson got the general idea. It was simply a pestle that pounded grain in a mortar-like hollow log or rock. This arrangement was on one end of a long pole; there was a post in the middle that acted as a balance. On the other end of the pole was a wooden bucket sort of contraption built with a slant towards the rear and with slits in the bottom that kept the box-like contraption from holding water for any length of time. This part of the "mill" sat under a drop of water from a small sluice of a small waterfall, and when the box filled with water, it went down, forcing the pestle at the other end of the pole to go up in the air over the grain to be pounded. Of course, when the water suddenly spilled out, it sent the pestle falling down with considerable force into the mortar and crushing the grain. The rebound shot the box back up under the flow of water, and of course, the operation was repeated, over and over, until the grain had been "ground" or pounded.

Nelson discussed the stars in the beautiful sky with Ben and found out that although they had different names for some of the constellations, their myths and legends were nearly always the same. Such was the case of the brightest star in the sky, Sirius, the dog star, which they both knew rose in conjunction with the sun and held the true meaning of the term "Dog Days."

As they talked, Nelson explained a feature that had puzzled his companion. Ben was fascinated with the new stove at the Tift home. This was merely an extension built through the wall and out the back of the fireplace from another room, through which hot coals and ashes could be pushed from the back of the fireplace, into a metal box-like container, sitting on two legs, in the next room. It was called a Pennsylvania Five Plate Stove and was not much more than a foot-warmer or fire box as far as Nelson was concerned. He told Ben that he thought the Franklyn Stove would be around a long time after this type of stove had gone out of style.

Ben got some water from the spring, and Nelson put some on the fire to heat so that he could take his usual Saturday night bath. Ben sat and watched his master take a "sponge" type bath with the hot soapy water and asked why folks took a bath on Saturday nights instead of another night.

"Ben, I think you have noticed that I let you work in the garden and do other work after sundown on the Sabbath day. The old folks established a rule long ago that the Sabbath starts after sundown on Saturday, and the Good Book tells us that 'Cleanliness is next to Godliness.' This is also found in the Hebrew testaments as cited by Phinehas Ben Yair as well as in a sermon by John Wesley. Ben, if we believe that the Sabbath starts after sundown on Saturday, then in order to be clean on the Lord's day, one must bathe after sundown on Saturday, and if there is work that needs to be done, it can be done after sundown on Sunday."

"Yassuh, Boss," Ben chuckled.

"Never mind that 'Yassuh, Boss' stuff. Do you understand what I am talking about?"

"Nawsuh, Boss, but it is easier to say 'Yassuh, Boss' than it is for you to go back through all that talk and then I still won't know what you mean."

"Ben?"

"Yassuh, Boss."

"Get this mess cleaned up and go on and go to sleep. I will take the first watch tonight."

"Yassuh, Boss."

Nelson laughed to himself. He knew that Ben was playing one of his little games with him and that Ben figured he had gotten the best of this exchange. But in this way, both men benefited and no harm was done.

It grew colder during the night, and Nelson was wrapped up in his blanket and hovering over the little fire when the time came to wake Ben. They camped that night near Byron and went on into Albany the next morning.

Nelson had the animals delivered to John Jackson with a note that read: "Dear John, I could not take these fine animals on board the 'Edwin Forest,' so as I had my new barouche on board, I decided to drive them from Columbus to Albany. I found them to be wonderfully trained and conditioned." John came straight from his place of business to see Nelson and thank him, but Nelson said, "Nonsense, John. You would have done the same for a friend. Old Ben and I had a capital adventure doing it."

The "Edwin Forest" arrived several days later, and the word went out in southwest Georgia and down to Apalachicola that the "Edwin Forest" was using a "black" pilot. Nelson knew that he would be criticized for breaking the color line in the steamboat business, but knew that, like all things, it would pass. It did, and soon some of the very men who had blamed Nelson for giving "Red Buck" a chance to show that he could handle a steamboat were heard to remark in taverns and saloons up and down the rivers, that they had known all along that old "Red Buck" had it in him. Of course, these same men were quick to add, "Of course, you do know that the red one has plenty of Creek Indian blood flowing in his veins, and they were the first river men of this area." Others hinted, "White folks down around Bainbridge know 'Red Buck' much better than others along the river, and they have every right. There might be more than Indian blood flowing in his veins and the folks in Bainbridge are sure to know as it might be some of theirs." Then the teller would lower his voice and look around to see if anyone could be listening in on his confidential story, adding mysteriously, "If'n you know what I mean?" Of course, this was followed by much nudging and sly winks between teller and listener.

Bad news was not long coming from Columbus. The Bank of Columbus was entering suit against Nelson for three thousand dollars. Mr. Stewart, the president of the bank, was disclaiming all knowledge of the agreement between his agents and Nelson Tift saying that his agents had exceeded their authority and had acted without consulting him. Nelson was also out his time, and the expense of making the trip to Columbus. He resolved not to take what he considered an insult to his intelligence and a smear on his integrity, lightly. "John, what do you think I should do in this instance?" he asked John Jackson one evening.

"Nelson, you have some very powerful and influential friends, and I have a few myself. You have never called on your friends to help you, and I know that you have an aversion to that sort of thing. But people like the Warrens, Tomlinson Fort, Jeptha C. Harris, General Brisbane and Jesse Mercer can be of service. Your business associates and close friends in Savannah, Augusta, Hawkinsville, and Milledgeville and all the friends here in southwest Georgia who know and love you would be hurt if you did not ask for their help when you feel that you are being ill-treated. Believe me, Nelson, when these bankers learn they are pressuring someone who has friends in high places, they back off rather than disturb the waters too much."

"You don't think my friends will feel that I am being presumptuous if I ask for their advice and perhaps a little help, if it comes to that?"

"Man, alive, Nelson. Men like Tomlinson Fort do not associate with men like Nelson Tift by accident. Tomlinson is a veteran of the War of 1812, the son of Arthur Fort of Warren County, Georgia, who served in the Revolutionary War. Tomlinson Fort is an author of a medical book, has practiced medicine for years, has served in Congress, founded a newspaper, is one of the founders of the first state medical school and of the first insane asylums in the country. Last but not least, he knows all about banks and banking and can help you in this matter."

On the seventh of November, 1840, Nelson was elected Colonel of the Baker County Regiment. Of course, the fact that he had been the organizer of the Augusta Guards was well known in southwest Georgia and had much to do with his being selected. The general public believed that the right man had been picked for the job, as Nelson's administrative ability and courage had been demonstrated time and again. People who had referred to Nelson as "Captain" Tift now referred to him as Colonel Tift. Nelson and Ben made a trip down to Newton to get a copy of the official orders and a roster of the men who had "signed up." On the way back home, rain started pouring down, and the two men got under the barouche, put their canvas across the seats and sat out the downpour. "Read me some of the mens who's in your army, Colonel," Ben asked as they sat huddled under the barouche.

"I'll do better than that if you will wait until we get back home. I will let you make your mark on the roster, and you will be a member of the Regiment," Nelson promised.

"Do that mean will I will shoot at folks, Colonel?"

"Perhaps, and it might mean that they will shoot at you."

"They gonna shoot at you, too?"

"I expect they will, but we must hope that our being prepared will deter any such an eventuality."

"Yassuh, Boss."

Nelson availed himself of the opportunity to purchase four Albany lots for three hundred dollars and to trade them a few days later to P. O. Clayton for a two thousand one hundred fifty-six dollars stock of goods tht Clayton was closing out. Charles and Nelson contracted to build three small houses and sold Barrett Taylor lot number fourteen on Pine Street for two hundred dollars. They sold lots eighteen and twenty on Flint Street, with improvements, for two hundred and fifty dollars each. Nelson made the remark while they were making the entries in the ledger, "Charles, I want to be very careful to hold off selling lots on the corners of the residential section that should be given for building churches. I want each child that might be born to Maria and me to have a corner lot to build their homes on someday." Charles went over to the plat book they used and blocked off some unsold corner lots they still controlled around Albany.

"Nelson, as of today, the twenty-first of November, 1840, the corner lots that you want to reserve have been so marked," Charles said after he had completed the task.

"Which reminds me, little brother, you are now over twenty-one years of age, and it is about time that you took on some property and the added responsibility that goes with it. Make out the proper deeds from me to you, of any ten lots of your choice in the town of Albany, that are unsold and to which I have clear title. These are my present to you for being so faithful."

Of course, Charles had known that one of these days his older brother would get around to doing exactly what he was now doing. Much water had gone under the bridge since he had joined his brother in Augusta. He had doubted him at times but was now convinced that although Nelson frequently lost a battle, he usually won the war. Charles carefully selected lots on Broad, Pine, Front, and North Streets. Nelson requested only one small change of the lots selected when Charles chose one lot on the corner of Pine and Washington, saying, "Select another elsewhere as that is the area where the big cotton warehouse is to be built."

Maria was worn out. She had a sick child, a stack of dirty clothes a mile high, and she was angry at some of her women friends about church work.

"I just declare, they know that I am up to my chin in work, and they just keep electing me and appointing me to this and that," she told Nelson in exasperation.

"You must learn to say 'no', my dear, and then they will not call on you so much after that," Nelson replied in a tired voice. Then he added, "Maria, I received notice today to appear at the Bank of Columbus to settle on a note of Shotwell and Tift with Mr. A. B. Davis, the bank cashier."

"Oh, I am so ashamed to be complaining with my little troubles when you have so many things on you. Please forgive your silly little wife," Maria said and went over to comfort her husband.

"I should have known better than to have dealings with underlings. I have written some letters and talked with some men that might have some influence on the outcome of this meeting in Columbus. Perhaps I can get things settled."

On the fifteenth of January, 1841, Nelson was re-elected Justice of the Inferior Court of Baker County. He had little opposition, as his had been a good administration and his record spoke for itself. Charles was against his brother's holding the office for another term. He knew that Nelson already had too many things on his mind and that even a man with a sturdy constitution and much ambition could work himself into an early grave. He had cautioned his brother repeatedly and had even mentioned it to his sister-in-law several times, saying, "If and when I go to Key West, who will take on all the responsibility he had put on himself and me?"

"I know, Charles, and I have told him the same thing time and again, but he just says that he will ease up presently," Maria said resignedly.

On the ninth of February, 1841, four thousand seven hundred dollars worth of town lots were sold to Shackleford and Gibbs. Two lots were sold to Mr. Massil on the same day for five hundred dollars. Mr. Gunnerson purchased two lots for six hundred, and two lots were sold to Mr. Gours for five hundred and fifty dollars. Doctor Cox purchased one lot for three hundred to be paid for in services. Amos Chapman Tift said he wanted to show his faith in his younger brother and the new town, so he sent one thousand, eight hundred thirty-six dollars to purchase twelve town lots.

"All of this goes on the credit side of the ledger, Charles," Nelson instructed as he looked up from the pile of papers and documents he had been reading. "Now put down eight hundred dollars paid to James Bond for the stock we purchased from him, on the debit side of the ledger."

"You know, Brother, there were two merchants in here from Americus yesterday who told me they were really beginning to feel the pinch the unreliable specie is causing," Charles said, and added, "Nelson, I thought you were making a mistake swapping paper for land, but I am sure happy now that we got rid of that trash."

"I think those visitors from Americus know whereof they speak for I have for some time felt the noose tightening on all specie. You know that I sure was glad to get that good hard money Amos Chapman sent for the land. I declare hard money these days is like a breath of fresh air to a person who has been confined to a dungeon for several days," Nelson asnwered ruefully.

Heavy rains had been falling for days, and the roads were now nearly impassable. Some of the bridges were out, and business was at a virtual standstill. Nelson, John Jackson, Doctor Gilbert, and Mr. Randall met together at Randall's and Grant's warehouse to discuss the high water and the threat of a real flood that hung over Albany like a great sword that would come down on them if it continued to rain.

"I tell you, gentlemen, my friend Harris has already gotten most of his warehouse stock moved out, and the water is now over a foot deep in there. Mr. Randall and I will have to evacuate this warehouse by the fifteenth of March, if the river crests higher than we have seen it before. It is within inches of that level at this moment," Mr. Grant said, shaking his head and spitting tobacco juice into three inches of water that already covered most of the dirt floor of the warehouse.

"Well, I suppose you think I gambled that the steamer 'Louisa' could make it to Apalachicola through these flooded waters with the five hundred bales of cotton from my warehouse, but gentlemen, I assure you that I would gladly make the same gamble again rather than sit here and wait for the cotton to float itself out of the warehouse and down into the swamps," John Jackson said, "however, today is the twelfth, and I believe that if the rain will cease by the fifteenth of March, we can still survive this crisis."

"The 'Louisa' is due back here by next Thursday, and if she is going to try to make another run, I am going to get everything I have sold and awaiting delivery on board her and out of here," said Mr. Harris.

"My, friends," said Nelson. "I know this is a most inappropriate time to hold a meeting to discuss the new railroad and the need for bridges when mere survival is uppermost in the minds of all. John, if you will just give us a status report regarding the building of the right-of-way roadbed, maybe it will get this infernal rain off our minds for a moment or so."

John Jackson rose to his feet and pulled some papers from the inside pocket of his coat.

"Well, boys, as Colonel Tift says, this is a bad time to have to stand up before you and give this report, but you have asked for it, and so here it is. Two hundred fifty thousand dollars worth of stock has been subscribed in the Ocmulgee and Flint Railroad. About fifteen percent of that amount is given in notes. The east half of the road is now under contract at fifteen cents per cubic yard, and the west half is to be advertised, and the contract let for grading on the fourth Saturday of April, 1841." John Jackson turned to Nelson and indicated that his report was ended.

"Thank you, John. Now, men, I know that you have all been subjected to the same barrage of criticism that I have been hearing from the opposition to having the railroad built. I know that this is a bad moment for one to show optimism, but nevertheless, I do believe that our detractors will be silenced by the progress being made and the unflinching course being pursued by the directors who met last week in Starksville and renewed their intentions to see the job done. I want to impress upon you that other interests are at work building railroads from Mobile east to where they are most needed and wanted. This same sort of extension of existing rail services is being offered to this section from the north. When these interests recognize that there is a real need for services down this way, so much so that we are building our own railroad, then these interests will be anxious to extend their railheads a little farther, so that they can service southwest Georgia. Then we will have ingress and egress to and from the Albany area by rail from all over the country."

On the fourteenth of March, 1841, William Mercer and his family were forced to leave their house and the steam sawmill near the river for fear of being swept away by the high water. Maria and Nelson insisted on the Mercers moving in with them in their new house, which was all but finished. The rising water was now far up in Randall and Grant's warehouse and quite deep in the Harris warehouse. Nelson told Charles, "A few feet higher and the county will be completely under water westward to Cooleewahee Creek." Ben came in to report that Mrs. Long and her family were stranded on their land two miles below Albany; the rising river had made their place into an island on which they were trapped. Nelson instructed Ben to get the big flat-bottomed bateau and to follow him as he led the way in the light canoe, down through the swollen waters to the Long place.

"Charles, you stay here and look after my family and the town property. Mrs. Long and her folks do not have much in the sense of worldly possessions, and it looks as if the flood will take what little they do have. They are good, hard-working, industrious people, and I will not be able to rest until Ben and I have rescued them and have made some effort to salvage some of their meager belongings."

Ben poled the big bateau slowly down the middle of Front Street following his master who was skillfully paddling along between trees away up ahead where Front Street ended in the forest. Ben soon found his master waiting for him at the edge of the deep forest, and they slowly wended their way between tall trees and over the tops of bushes. They saw many animals and snakes up in the trees trying to ride out the flood. They also saw some livestock that had been swept away and drowned by the swift water. Several chickens were perched in the trees, and they saw some deer and a cow whose necks or backs had been broken when they were swept into an overhanging limb in which their horns had caught. They passed several farm houses and barns that were standing in several feet of water. There was no sign of life, and Nelson felt sure they had gotten away to higher ground before the water took their homes. There was less than an acre of dry land left above water level on the Long place. The mother, a fifteen-year-old boy, a twelve-year-old girl, and their old grandfather were standing on the porch straining their eyes toward the men in the two boats approaching them.

"It's Colonel Tift and old Ben, Mama," shouted the boy excitedly and ran out into the water and the drizzling rain to help the two men drag the prows of their boats up on the shore which was now licking at the front steps.

"Mrs. Long, take everything that you think we can get in the big boat. Grandfather Long, you and the boy get long sticks or sturdy poles from somewhere and get gloves or even heavy rags as Ben and I already have blisters on our hands, and we will be fighting the current going back to Albany. Everyone must hurry as we don't have much time. No, Mrs. Long, not the stove; we cannot possibly take things like that, and it will not float away. Just food, clothing, blankets, some cooking utensils, and some light housekeeping things will take up all the available space. That's right, young lady, right here in the boat. Now, Grandfather, you and your granddaughter will be in the little boat with me. Mrs. Long, you and your son will go in the bateau with Ben."

It took them only ten minutes to make their choice of what they would put in the boats and what they would abandon to the whim of the flood. Once the boats were loaded with the bare necessities and a few things of sentimental value, they took leave of their home. Mrs. Long looked back over her shoulder only one time at the forlorn, lonely, brave little house that now timidly stood with its foundation in the muddy, swirling flood. It was nearly dark when they saw the first roof top on Front Street through the now steady drizzle, and in a few more minutes more they heard a voice calling, "Colonel Tift! Ben! Nelson Tift! Ben!" over and over, and they knew that the folks up there on the high ground at the corner of Front and Broad were getting worried about them. The hands of Colonel Tift and Ben were now raw and bleeding. Those miserable beings in the boats were soaking wet, but they could now see the outlines of people running around carrying lamps and fat pine torches.

Willing hands pulled the Long children, their mother, and the exhausted but game old man from the half-filled, waterlogged boats. Maria had made the necessary arrangements with some of her good church women friends and the Longs, with their pile of goods, were taken by willing hands to places of warmth and love. Nelson and Ben went to the house where Mrs. Mercer and Annie Maria put soothing salves on blistered hands. Both men were exhausted, but they had that wonderful feeling of having done a good deed and having done it well. Grandfather Long told the people with whom he was staying that Colonel Tift was like an angel from the Lord who had appeared just as they had despaired of any relief from the rising waters. Mrs. Long told all who would listen to her how gentle, strong, and brave Old Ben had been in the big bateau.

"With his pore hands ableeding and already so tired that he could hardly talk, still he tried to save my little boy from getting his hands blistered and took off his coat and put it over me. I'll tell anybody that I love and respect old Ben above many a white folks I know."

The flood was over, the waters had receded, all except in the low places where wagon loads of fish were being caught in seines. A person could buy a "croker" bag full for little or nothing. Beautiful arrowheads and other Indian artifacts had been washed up out of the Flint and deposited in the low places, and small boys and girls raced to find these curiosities. Nelson saw a man with a fifty-pound sturgeon. There were many catfish that large or larger while fifteen-pound trout were commonplace and were for the taking from the little low ponds that were rapidly disappearing. All of the bridges on the Kinchafoonee and Muckalee Creeks had been swept away. To add to the troubled times that confronted the little town and its inhabitants, a fire broke out on the high ground, and the men of Albany worked so hard to put out the blaze that their hands became as blistered as those of Ben and Nelson had been from their rescue of the Long family.

Flood reports drifted in from Columbus, Fort Gaines, Eufaula, Georgetown, Bainbridge, and Newton. All of these places and many others had been hard hit by the flood. Albany had been able to hold onto its three steam sawmills, but a rebuilding effort had to be begun immediately, for there was no way in or out of the town except by boat. Bridges and roads had to be repaired or rebuilt. Many homes had to be repaired or rebuilt in their entirety. The sawmills were put into operation, and the people began to clean up and rebuild the bridges, their homes and business houses.

* * * * *

The biographical novel is a child of history and fiction. It attempts to tell the story of its main character in essence, recreating the individual against the background of his times. The accounts of events found in the *Gentle Connecticut Georgian* trilogy, of which this book is Volume II, is a result of the author's intensive study of records pertaining to the area and persons depicted. Readers interested in sources and background may contact the author for reference to specific interviews, notes and other material.